The Extralateral Right in the Mining Law

Shall It Be Abolished?

by Wm. E. Colby

with an introduction by Kerby Jackson

GOLD RUSH BOOKS

OREGON, USA

www.GoldMiningBooks.com

Introduction

It has often been said that "*gold is where you find it*", but even beginning prospectors understand that their chances for finding something of value in the earth or in the streams of the Golden West are dramatically increased by going back to those places where gold and other minerals were once mined by our forerunners. Despite this, much of the contemporary information on local mining history that is currently available is mostly a result of mere local folklore and persistent rumors of major strikes, the details and facts of which, have long been distorted. Long gone are the old timers and with them, the days of first hand knowledge of the mines of the area and how they operated. Also long gone are most of their notes, their assay reports, their mine maps and personal scrapbooks, along with most of the surveys and reports that were performed for them by private and government geologists. Even published books such as this one are often retired to the local landfill or backyard burn pile by the descendents of those old timers and disappear at an alarming rate. Despite the fact that we live in the so-called "Information Age" where information is supposedly only the push of a button on a keyboard away, true insight into mining properties remains illusive and hard to come by, even to those of us who seek out this sort of information as if our lives depend upon it. Without this type of information readily available to the average independent miner, there is little hope that our metal mining industry will ever recover.

This important volume and others like it, are being presented in their entirety again, in the hope that the average prospector will no longer stumble through the overgrown hills and the tailing strewn creeks without being well informed enough to have a chance to succeed at his ventures.

Kerby Jackson
Josephine County, Oregon
May 2018

CONTENTS

California Law Review

| Volume IV. | JULY, 1916 | Number 5 |

The Extralateral Right: Shall It Be Abolished?*

THERE is no feature of the American mining law that has provoked more spirited discussion and against which a greater amount of criticism has been aimed than the extralateral right, or "law of apex," or dip right, as it is variously termed. It has become quite popular to present the arraignment of charges which can legitimately be made against the practical operation of this right and there is scarcely a meeting of importance connected with the mining industry where some one does not add to this volume of condemnation. In all this discussion, it is rare to find a word of commendation and not only are the advantages which flow from the exercise of this right ignored, but in the general demand for its abolition we find very little well considered thought given to the serious results of such action and few suggestions as to what steps should be taken to minimize the grave consequences which are bound to follow such a radical and far reaching change in our mining law. We are too prone to assume that legislation is a panacea for all defects in existing laws and not enough attention is paid to the evils which inevitably flow from "half baked" remedial statutes. Judging from the published remarks of many who have criticized the extralateral right, the opinion seems to be quite prevalent that all that is necessary to be done to cure the ills that are inherent in the "law of apex" is for Congress to pass a statute abolishing it.

It is not the purpose of this article to attempt to demonstrate that the extralateral right feature should be retained in our mining laws. It may well be that should the right be abolished, a satisfactory solution of the difficulties which must be met can

---

* There are several bills to amend our mining laws pending before the present Congress. One of these would abolish the extralateral right without any provisions to relieve the serious consequences of such action. This discussion is prompted by this proposed revision.

be reached. But this article is written in the hope that it may correct some of the misinformation which has been circulated concerning the subject and unfortunately generally accepted, and also to point out a few of the problems which must inevitably be dealt with in a satisfactory way if we are to avoid placing ourselves in a worse position than we now occupy.

With this object in view, the subject will be presented in the following manner:

First: From a comparative standpoint, treating of the existence of the extralateral right in the mining laws of other countries.

Second: From a historical standpoint, treating of the origin, growth and development of the right in the United States.

Third: From an analytical standpoint, setting forth the arguments for and against the right and the consequences which must follow its abolition.

I. COMPARATIVE TREATMENT

In a discussion of this character it is interesting to know whether other systems of mining law have similar features and what has been the result of their operation. It has been erroneously assumed by many that the extralateral right is a unique burden suffered by the United States alone. An examination of the laws of other countries shows that this is not a fact. Naturally we cannot expect to find in other countries an extralateral law identical in all respects with our own. It is the fundamental principle underlying this law that is vital,[1] viz: the right to mine on and pursue a vein in depth beneath surface ground that is not owned or controlled by the mine operator. In other words, the right to follow the vein in depth is independent of and is not measured by surface ownership, hence it is termed the right of extralateral pursuit. It is usually described as being opposed in principle to the common law idea of ownership of land, where the owner of the surface is entitled to everything situated vertically beneath. As Judge Lindley has pointed out in his treatise on the Law of Mines[2] the common law

---

[1] "The application of the term 'extralateral' to this right is of comparatively recent origin and the right existed long prior to this designation." Lindley on Mines, 3d Ed. § 568.

[2] Lindley on Mines, 3d Ed. § 568.

recognized the right of severance and frequently the surface owner conveyed to another the right to mine a vein or mineral bearing strata that penetrated or lay beneath his surface. However, the extralateral right as we ordinarily conceive of it has an element that did not exist in the common law. In the exercise of the extralateral right the vein may be pursued *indefinitely* in depth beneath the surface of adjoining owners who have nothing to say about the exercise of this right underneath their ground and are powerless to prevent it. The right has been created by statute or custom before their surface ownership attached and the vein has been reserved and carved out of their estate. It is the statutory or customary origin of the right, giving it an indefinite sweep in depth and the fact that it is not at all dependent upon conveyance from private owners of overlying surface, nor for its measurement upon the vertical boundaries of such surface ownership that distinguishes the extralateral right from the common law severance of minerals from the surface.

We have no definite information as to whether an extralateral right was exercised in ancient times. The existing record of these ancient mining laws is meager and a great part of the mining was carried on as a sovereign venture so that the question of extralateral pursuit would seldom arise.[3] It is only when there are adjoining private ownerships that a situation is created where the question becomes important.

Under the democratic control of Athens the silver-lead mines of Mt. Laurion were leased in small adjoining areas to individuals. One might expect to find the extralateral right a feature of the Ancient Greek mining law were it not for the fact that these were flat lying contact deposits occupying horizontal beds and hence unsuited to the exercise of any dip right.[4]

Germany and Austria. The first recorded appearance of the extralateral right, so far as the writer is aware, was in the year 1249, and is contained in a code of mining law proclaimed for the mining town of Iglau by the King of Bohemia. By its terms the discoverer of a mine "shall have by right in that which is commonly called the roof (hanging wall of vein), three and a half

---

[3] Those interested in the subject of Ancient Mining Laws will find an excellent note at pp. 82-86 of Hoover's translation of Agricola, De Re Metallica.

[4] See Hoover's Agricola, p. 83 footnote.

Lehen (an ancient Germanic measure) and in that which is called foot (wall of vein), one *Lehen*, in height and depth in equal proportions." In the event of a dispute between two adjoining claimants the matter was submitted to an impartial jury of four and if necessary to determine whether a trespass was committed or not the two workings were required to be connected. Many will recognize in this the litigation work which has become such a pronounced feature of our modern extralateral cases.[5]

It is in the mining districts of the various states that afterwards became merged in the Germanic and Austrian Empires that the extralateral law or right to follow the vein indefinitely in depth had its earliest and most complete development. The right was founded on ancient custom and its origin is lost in the obscurity which surrounded the early beginnings of mining in those regions. It later became crystallized and confirmed in the charters and proclamations issued by the various kings and rulers of these states. There is a remarkable similarity running through these various laws in force in the different districts and while details differ they give evidence of having been impressed with the same ideas which were doubtless traceable to a common origin.[6]

The extralateral right in force in these Germanic States was complex in the extreme.[7] There were two general classes of mining claims. The *Längenfeld*, sometimes called the *Gestecktes-*

---

[5] The writer acknowledges his indebtedness to Mr. Herbert C. Hoover for the permission to use the foregoing information which Mr. Hoover collated from Geschichte des Bergbaues, etc., Vol. II, pp. 14-35 (1838) by Kaspar von Sternberg; Dr. J. A. Tomaschek. Das Alte Bergrecht von Iglau, pp. 3-10 (1897), and Geschichte der Böhmischen und Mährischen Bergwerke by J. T. Perthner, (Wien, 1780).

[6] In this respect these mining laws bear a striking resemblance to the miners' rules and regulations which sprang up in the Western States following the discovery of gold in 1848. They were founded on custom and as they spread through the other mining regions from their source in California they were modified in details but retained similar fundamental principles.

[7] The writer is indebted to his wife, Rachel Vrooman Colby, and to Mr. W. J. Aschenbrenner for invaluable assistance in the translation of the Germanic authorities which form the source for this presentation. Some idea of the difficulties encountered in translating the Old German works may be gained from the fact that ten different German dictionaries devoted exclusively to mining terms were consulted. The German works consulted are: Die Vermessung der Längenfelder, by von Hatzfeld, Oberbergamtsmarkscheider in Bonn, published in Zeitschrift für Bergrecht, (1899), Vol. 40, pp. 418-441; Commentar über das Bergrecht, by Chr. G. H. Hake (1823); Anleitung zu den Rechten und der Verfassung bey dem Bergbaue im Königreiche Sachsen, by Köhler (1824); De jure Quadraturae Metallicae, by S. A. W. Herder

feld or *Streichendesfeld*, because the claims were measured along the strike of the vein by long measure or *Längenmass*, was the class of mining claim which exercised the extralateral right. The *Geviertefeld* or *Seifenfeld* or *Quadratmass*, was a squared claim which was bounded by vertical planes passed through its exterior surface lines. The latter class of claims was employed to cover placer deposits and mineral deposits of great width with no regular strike or dip and also flat or bedded veins called *Flötze* which dipped at an angle of 20° or less, measured from the horizontal.[8]

The measuring or squaring (*Vierung*) of the *Längenfeld*[9] and of its extralateral right was an involved process. There was first a temporary or superficial measurement to fix approximately the boundaries so that other prospectors might know what ground was free to locate. When demand was made by a claimant or his adjoining owners, and the mine workings sufficiently extended to enable the measurements to be made, the formal squaring took place which established the boundaries definitely and finally. The surveyor first determined the main strike of the vein and marked this line out on the surface. The discovery shaft was the customary starting point and an attempt made to average the natural changes of the strike of the vein, usually resulting in an assumed middle line from which the lateral measurements of the surface boundaries were made.[10] An equal distance was thus measured each way along the top or apex of the vein from the discovery point and the two terminal or end points of the length taken on the vein marked. These *Längenfelder* varied in length in different mining districts. As a rule the *Fundgrube* or discoverer's claim was 42 *Lachters* in length and adjoining claims or *Massen* 28 *Lachters.*. The total legal width of the claim on the surface was

---

(1839). These are the recognized authorities on the German extralateral right. Other authorities too numerous to mention were also consulted. There has been very little material descriptive of the Germanic extralateral right published in English. Raymond in his excellent review of the mining laws of the world appearing in Mineral Resources, 1869, Part II, "Relations of Government to Mining," pp. 173-250 memtions it briefly, p. 195.

[8] In some districts the angle was 12° and in others 15°.

[9] The measuring of the claim was called the "Vierung" or squaring of the claim because the unit of measurement was usually a "Lehen", an ancient measure which was a square measuring 7 "Lachters" each way.

[10] This is somewhat analagous to the "lode line" of American mining locations.

usually *7 Lachters,*[11] which was divided either equally on each side of the vein, or the entire width could be taken on one side in special districts. The measurements were usually made from the walls of the vein, leaving the vein free in the middle, though in earlier times they were made from the middle of the vein. This was called the squaring of the claim and must not be confused with the squaring of the vein itself which was a distinct measurement. The squaring of the claim resulted in a definition of the surface area which the claimant was entitled to control.[12]

After a squaring of the claim on the surface had taken place it was necessary to determine what was the measure of the right to mine on the vein extralaterally. The longitudinal limits of this extralateral right were variously determined. There seems to have been a lack of explicit legal regulation of the manner in which this should be done and few data are found in the literature on this subject so that in practice much doubt and many conflicting views arose as to which legal principles should apply.[13] The procedure of measurement varied with the conception of the principle adopted in each case. The measurement most commonly employed was to pass a vertical plane through each marked end point of the vein at the linear extremities of the claim and at right angles to the general line of strike or average course of the vein, and extended into depth. These parallel planes constituted the longitudinal boundaries or end line planes of the *Längenfeld,* between which the vein could be worked extralaterally and to infinite depth.[14]

---

[11] A "Lachter" is 67.5 inches. Hoover's Agricola, note p. 78.

[12] Those who are familiar with the early mining history in the Western states of the United States will appreciate that this fundamental idea, so prominent in the measuring of the claim in Germany, of having the right to a certain length of vein which should control the laying out of the surface boundaries was quite widely accepted as being in force here. (Lindley on Mines, §§ 59, 573). Later the courts held that the actual position of the vein did not control the boundaries and the locator was only entitled to whatever length of vein he included within his surface lines. (Flagstaff Min. Co. v. Tarbet (1878), 98 U. S. 463, 25 L. Ed. 253). In Germany the vein remained the controlling element until a formal squaring of the claim had taken place which might not be for several years. In the United States the surface boundaries became the prime factor and the acquisition of the vein was subordinated to those boundaries.

[13] It is interesting to note that also in England the mining laws of Derbyshire and in the United States the mining Act of 1866 both failed to prescribe any rule for establishing the longitudinal or end boundaries of the extralateral segment of vein that attached to a mining claim.

[14] It is a striking coincidence that under the Act of 1866 where no specific provision was made for measuring the extralateral right the

Another measurement employed in some instances was called the Ball or Waterdrop method. This limitation was ascertained by passing vertical planes through the lines which would be established if we imagine the path of a ball or drop of water running down the plane of the inclined vein from each of the end points of the claim. If the strike of the vein changed materially in depth this would naturally produce curved or bent bounding planes. Another method consisted in ascertaining the end points of the lode at the surface by measuring out the length of the claim in both directions from the discovery point, following the lode in all its windings and variations, for this purpose, and then projecting these end points downward from level to level using the true dip of the vein to determine the projection. By connecting this series of projected end points the longitudinal boundary of the extralateral right was ascertained. There were still other methods used for determining the end boundaries but in modern times the measuring of these at right angles to the main or average line of strike became the general rule.[15]

The squaring of the vein or lode itself added to these complications. This squaring was considered much more important and was given preference over the squaring of the claim, for the latter had more to do with fixing surface boundaries. The square of the vein or deposit accompanied the lode in depth in all its variations and directions and at an equal distance therefrom. If we imagine two planes, one on each side of the vein and equidistant from it and following it in all its undulations and turnings in both strike and dip into unlimited depth we have the artificial limits within which the miner could mine and follow his main vein and if his claim was the senior in time he was entitled to any other veins or portions of veins which happened to exist between these artificial

---

American courts arrived independently at the same general result. Mr. Justice Field in Eureka, etc. Co. v. Richmond, etc., Co. (1877), 4 Sawyer 302, Fed. Cas. No. 4548, said: "Lines drawn vertically down through the ledge or lode, at right angles with a line representing this general course (of the vein) at the ends of the claimant's line of location, will carve out, so to speak, a section of the ledge or lode, within which he is permitted to work, and out of which he cannot pass." And Mr. Justice Temple in Argonaut Min. Co. v. Kennedy Min., etc., Co. (1900), 131 Cal. 15, 28, 63 Pac. 148, 82 Am. St. Rep. 317, used the following language: "Planes through the lode at the end lines of the location at right angles to the general course would impose the required limitation upon the rights of the locator along the lode."

[15] Zeitschrift für Bergrecht, Vol. 40 (1899), pp. 430-431.

bounding planes. If at any particular place in the main vein it became necessary to ascertain where these imaginary boundaries would fall, a point was taken on the wall of the vein and a straight line passed through it conforming to the general dip of the wall of the vein at that place and there was also passed through the same point and at right angles to the dip line a straight line conforming to the general strike of the vein at that place. At the point of intersection of these dip and strike lines a third line perpendicular to both the others was erected and extended out into the country rock away from the wall of the vein for the lawful distance and the extremity of this line would give the position of one of the imaginary bounding planes of the Längenfeld at that particular point. In other words the width of the territory within which the miner was permitted to work in his extralateral mining was measured from each wall of the vein out into the country rock and at right angles to the wall. This distance was commonly 3½ "Lachter" in the hanging and the same distance in the foot, i. e., on each side of the vein. In some districts the entire width could be taken on one side of the vein. The total width varied from 7 even up to 500 "Lachter" in some cases. Usually where the width was great it was measured from the vein on a horizontal plane instead of perpendicularly from the walls of the vein. The intersection, branching, faulting, pinching out of lodes within these imaginary planes and the consequent conflicts which arose between junior and senior extralateral claimants gave rise to the innumerable law suits and vexations litigation which finally resulted in the abolition of this class of claims.

In the case of the *Geviertefelder* or squared claims with vertical boundaries, mining was sometimes confined within these vertical limits to a particular vein or bedded deposit with the right to mine a specified distance into the hanging and foot walls and the right to mine on underlying or overlying veins granted to other claimants. Complications naturally arose in such cases when the identity of the particular deposit was doubtful or destroyed, etc., and claimants of other deposits contested the right to continue mining.

There is a general impression that the extralateral right is a thing of the past in Germany. It is true that in many of the mining districts the extralateral right was abolished commencing in the early part of the nineteenth century and that the general mining law of June 24, 1865, operated to abolish it completely, but existing vested rights were recognized. Owners of these *Längen-felder* carrying extralateral rights were given the privilege of changing to *Geviertefelder* or claims with vertical boundaries. In spite of the fact that the procedure for making the change was simple, many *Längenfelder* claimants either did not desire to make the change or were unable to do so because their claims were so situated with reference to one another that it was impossible to readjust them. As a consequence, there are still in existence in Germany today thousands of claims possessing extralateral rights and complicated cases involving the exercise of these rights are of not infrequent occurrence. As one of the writers on this subject states, "This is the inevitable result of the characteristic legal nature of the *Längenfeld* and its dependence on the changes of the deposit."[16] It is his opinion that while these claims may have had some usefulness under simple mining conditions, the incalculable changes in strike and dip of the mineral deposits gave rise to an excessive number of controversies and finally brought about the abolition of the law granting these rights so far as concerned initiating new rights.

This action of the Germanic States in abolishing the extra-lateral form of claim after it had been in operation for over six centuries is cited as one of the strongest arguments in favor of similar action being taken by the United States. While there are the same general underlying reasons here for such a change, any-one familiar with the German form of extralateral right with its much greater complexities and its earlier indefiniteness with regard to its longitudinal measurement in depth will appreciate that there was far greater justification for such action in Germany. The American extralateral law with all its complexities is compara-tively simple. Here we have surface claims the boundaries of which are defined and which only depend in a minor degree upon the position of the mineral deposit. Subsequent development showing that the claim does not conform to the position of the vein will not necessitate readjustment of boundaries.[17] Under the Germanic law, the surface boundaries of the claim were usually

---

[16] Zeitschrift für Bergrecht (1899), p. 419. The measuring of Läng-enfelder, by von Hatzfeld, Mining Surveyor General in Bonn. There are ten mining districts in this jurisdiction where there are extensive mining operations being carried on in these Längenfelder there being over 3000 in the jurisdiction of this Surveyor General alone.

[17] Harper v. Hill (1911), 159 Cal. 250, 113 Pac. 162.

dependent upon the ascertained position of the apex which might take years to establish, and meanwhile the claim was for its greater part a "float." Provision was made for a temporary ascertainment of boundaries but this only added to the complexity as the temporary survey yielded to the later permanent measurement. The rules for ascertainment of boundaries in the event the vein pinched out or split into branches or was faulted were also so involved that there is not space to discuss these complex and intricate features. Anyone familiar with the many intricacies and indeterminate features connected with the ascertainment of the Germanic extralateral right will appreciate that the American law with its definitely fixed surface boundaries and well defined extralateral planes passed through parallel end lines is simple by comparison.

France. The extralateral right does not appear to have obtained a pronounced hold on the mining law of France though it existed there in a modified degree in the early days of mining under customary rights.[18] Aguillon says this system of granting inclined locations was abandoned in France in 1810.[19] However, while the mining law of the Empire, April 21st, 1810, provided that in general the limits of a mining concession were to be fixed by vertical planes passed through a perimeter laid out on the surface,[20] there was nothing in the act to prevent their being inclined according to the formation of the deposit. The concessions may be granted by beds, i. e. following bedded and inclined deposits but this was not considered as regular.[21] Concessions of this character were granted in conformity to the "prejudices and very unfortunate customs" of one of the mining districts—that of Jemmapes.[22]

While the extralateral right did not appear in France except in the cases noted, yet it is clear that the fundamental principle underlying this right, viz: the severance of the mineral from the surface was one of the prime characteristics of French mining law.

---

[18] The writer is indebted to his wife for a portion of the translation of the material which forms the basis for this discussion.

[19] Legislation des Mines, Etrangere (1891), Vol. II, p. 48.

[20] The Act itself provides that vertical bounding planes must be adopted "unless the circumstances and localities require another mode of limitation," Title IV, Section I, rule 29.

[21] Halleck's De Fooz on the Law of Mines (1860), p. 120.

[22] Exposition of the Law of 1810 by Count Regnault de Saint Jean-D'Angely. De Fooz, appendix C, pp. 250-251.

The philosopher Turgot in a periodical of 1769,[23] urged that each land owner as a matter of natural equity should have the right to mine on his own ground and then to pass underneath in the subsoil of his neighbor without the latter's consent and become the owner of the material which he extracted therefrom.[24] Dupont criticizes this system as an application to the mining industry of the celebrated doctrine of *laissez faire* which would result in the most complete anarchy—a true subterranean war.[25] Curvelier criticizes the system as utopian.[26]

Practically all of the French philosophers and statesmen who have expressed themselves on the subject agree that there is nothing in common as far as ownership of the surface and of the mineral underneath is concerned. De Fooz says: The "nature of things", the "general principles of right", and "general utility" do not permit the surface to be confounded with that which is beneath. The surface may be divided *ad infinitum* and this renders its culture easier and more productive but mines are not divisible like the surface and their occurrence has nothing in common with the configuration of the surface.[27] Jousselin says mines have a conformation of their own which in no way depends upon the character of the surface and can be worked to advantage when they are treated in mass or in sections of certain extent, without reference to surface boundaries.[28] A vein which forms a mine may extend into the depth of the earth a considerable distance beneath surface properties infinitely divided among the surface owners. Which one of these surface owners ought to have the property in the vein? It is necessary in order to work mines to advantage to treat mines *in mass*, or in sections of definite extent determined by the position and character of the beds or veins.[29] Mirabeau concluded one of the most famous debates on the fundamental principles of a true property in mines which took place in the French Chamber of Deputies in 1791 by saying: "The oblique direction of a mine may in a short distance pass underneath a

---

[23] Memoire au Conseil d'Etat.
[24] Naudier, Legislation des Mines (1877), p. 38.
[25] Dupont, Legislation des Mines (1862), Vol. I, p. 5.
[26] Curvelier, Legislation Miniere (1902), p. 5.
[27] Halleck's De Fooz, p. 10.
[28] Traite des servitudes d'utilite publique.
[29] Report of Count Girardin on the Law of 1810. De Fooz, p. 10, note 2, and Appendix D, p. 259.

hundred different properties. We already know too well the scourge of war upon the surface of the globe; there is no need of adding to it the scourge of a subterranean war."[30] He also argued that the proprietary right of the surface owner could not possibly apply to minerals several hundred feet in depth. "They cannot be a complement to the soil, and are moreover, by their course, unfit to be included in a partition of the surface." He pointed out the fact that the surface proprietor seldom had the capital to develop a mine and if he did he might find the valuable part of the vein to be under his neighbor's property.[31] The surface overlying a mine may be fertile or barren, cultivated or unculti- vated and the owner thereof has done absolutely nothing towards the acquisition, increase or creation of the mineral wealth con- cealed thereunder.[32] De Fooz, therefore, concludes that as a matter of art, of right, and of interest the regalian doctrine ought to prevail over the narrow principle of private ownership and that mines and the outcrops of mines, i. e., the points where they rise to the soil belong to the nation rather than to the surface pro- prietor.[33]

Napoleon at first opposed this idea because he interpreted article 552 of his famous Civil Code to grant to the proprietor of the surface everything beneath and the doctrine of a national property in mines would violate this principle of private ownership which he had already promulgated. The counter arguments advanced in the Council of State and already noted finally pre- vailed and in order to avoid the acknowledgment of defeat the Emperor resorted to a fiction, entirely his own,[34] "that mines are a new property; the right of working them forms a new wealth; and the property of mines does not exist prior to their concession." The famous French Law of Mines of April 21st, 1810, was the out- come.[35] The surface proprietor was recognized, however, for he

---

[30] De Fooz, p. 10, note 4 and p. 13.
[31] Foreign Mining Laws, Vol. II, Part I, Transactions of the Min- ing Association and Institute of Cornwall (1888), pp. 35-36.
[32] Compte, de la Propriete, De Fooz, p. 11, note 6.
[33] p. 13.
[34] A "real property separated from the surface is a conception abso- lutely new, which emanated from the genius who consolidates and aggrandizes each day the destinies of France." Report of Count Stan- islas Girardin, Appendix D, Halleck's De Fooz, p. 266.
[35] De Fooz, pp. 37-42.

was paid a small royalty or rental depending upon the area of surface required for successful operation.

As a result of the careful analysis of underlying principles and searching debate which preceded the adoption of the French Mining Law by the Chamber of Deputies, it is ideal from a theoretical standpoint. The mineral deposit is a property distinct from the overlying surface and the Council of Mines determines in each case, from the evidence produced, whether it should give preference in the granting of a concession to the discoverer, or the proprietor of the surface or to another applicant. The person or company best qualified to undertake the venture usually received the concession. The extent of the concession, within a maximum limitation, depended upon the character of the deposit and was determined largely by economy of operation. A perimeter was marked out on the surface and the concessionaire operated on the vein or mineral deposit within vertical planes passed through this perimeter. The owners of the surface within the perimeter continued to cultivate or use the surface except such portions as were required for actual mining operations and for which portions compensation was paid. Other veins or bedded deposits within the perimeter might be excluded and granted to other parties, as the concession usually carried the right to mine only on one particular deposit or vein. When a concessionaire had mined to the limit of his concession an extension of the perimeter was usually granted him since economy of operation justified such a course. It will be apparent that these advantages of granting concessions to those best qualified to undertake the venture and of making the extent of the concession dependent solely upon the character and occurrence of the deposit which was consequently not forced into claims of uniform and unvarying size and likely to be unsuited to the particular deposit is perfect in conception. This system embodies a fundamental feature of the extralateral right, viz: the right to mine on the vein without acquisition of surface ownership. While the other characteristic feature of indefinite pursuit of the vein in depth is lacking, the right to extend his perimeter in that direction was invariably granted to the concessionaire whose workings were most favorably situated for economic mining.

While this system is ideal, considered from most angles, yet like many ideal systems its successful operation depends upon ideal circumstances. In a country like France, thickly populated and with mining confined to comparatively well defined areas such a paternalistic surveillance as is exercised by the Council of Mines and the Engineers of Mines probably yields the best results, but in the Western part of the United States where the mining districts are sparsely settled and largely in remote and rugged regions, such a system would be impossible of administration. Walmesley says that the principal objection to the French system is "too much State control."[36] It is an interesting commentary on the urgent demand for a change in our mining laws to note that in 1889 a Commission of Deputies reported to the Chamber on the subject of revision of the French Mining law that the main object of legislation should be to free the mine owner of state control as much as possible; that England and the United States are in the almost complete possession of a law as wise in its simplicity as that which they indicate as the perfection of mining law; that everywhere the power of the State in such matters is being restrained; and that everywhere greater belief is being placed in private enterprise and industrial liberty and that it is a remarkable fact that the more this faith increases the more mineral wealth is developed.[37] The policy of severing the mineral from the surface and disposing of each separately is a most desirable feature, however, and it is regrettable that it was not adopted in the United States in the infancy of mining here.[38]

England. In the main, the law of England on the subject of mines did not recognize any severance of the vein from the surface. The surface owner was entitled to everything found vertically beneath his surface, except royal mines, i.e. mines of precious metals, and these latter were of little importance in England. There were some noteworthy exceptions, however.

In Derbyshire there existed a local mining law which was the outgrowth of ancient customs and regulations adopted by the miners themselves. It marked a wide departure from the ordinary conception of common law property rights. Under this law

---

[36] Mining Laws of the World (1894), p. 50.
[37] Walmesley, Mining Laws of the World, p. 52.
[38] The severance of mineral from the surface and the policy of disposing of each separately has recently been adopted by the Federal Government in the case of public lands valuable for oil, coal, phosphates, nitrates, potash, gas, and asphaltic deposits, etc. See 38 Stat. at L. 509; 35 Stat. at L. 844; 36 Stat. at L. 583; 37 Stat. at L. 105; 38 Stat. at L. 335; 37 Stat. at L. 497; and 37 Stat. at L. 687.

the miner had a right to enter upon privately owned lands within certain districts to "dig, delve, subvert, mine, turn up all manner of Grounds, Lands, Meadows, Closes, Pastures, Moors or Marshes for Lead-ore . . . . dwelling-houses, Highways, Orchards or Gardens excepted."[39] The first finder (discoverer) of a vein was entitled to two meers or measures along the vein and the lord who owned the ground to one meer and each locator thereafter to one meer. These meers were linear measurements along the apex of the vein at the surface and in different districts varied from 27, 29, 31, to 32 yards in length. Meer stakes at each end served to mark the possession. The width of the claim was a quarter cord or quarter meer measured either from the skirts (walls) of the vein or, according to the contention of the owner of the land, from the center of the vein.[40] Within this width the miner had the right to erect necessary mine buildings, store ore and waste, but all of this width that he did not need for these purposes belonged to the owner of the surrounding land for "it is not the land, but the necessary privilege of working the mine that is granted the miner."[41] Some have questioned whether an extralateral right was granted by these customs and while there is no explicit language contained in any of the Articles to indicate that such is the fact, nevertheless their examination leads to the unquestionable conclusion that such a right did exist. The Articles provide for litigation work, inspection of adjoining mines to ascertain if a trespass has been committed, and penalty for trespass on another claimant's forefield. The descriptions of dialling (surveying) to ascertain whether a claimant had reached the limit of his possession also indicate the existence of the right. From these descriptions it is evident that the longitudinal limit of the extralateral right in depth is measured by vertical planes passed through each end of the claim at right

---

[39] Houghton, Rara Avis in Terris or The Compleat Miner (1681), p. 14. For additional information regarding these unique laws see: The Compleat Mineral Laws of Derbyshire, Steer (1734); A Collection of Scarce and Valuable Treatises on Mines, etc., Payne (1738); The Miner's Guide, Hardy (1748); The Rhymed Chronicle by Manlove, etc., Tapping's edition (1851); Fodinae Regales, Pettus (1670); Bainbridge on Mines and Minerals, 6th ed. (1900); MacSwinney on Mines, 3rd ed. (1907).

[40] It is interesting to note that the identical dispute as to the measurement of the width of the claim existed in Germany. Hake, Bergrecht, p. 146.

[41] Mander's Derbyshire Miners' Glossary, p. 56.

angles to the general course of the vein.[42] The whole matter is set at rest, however, by the testimony of the barmasters or head mining officials given before the Royal Commission on Mining Royalties in 1891. The barmaster[43] of the wapentake of Wirksworth or Low Peak in Derbyshire was asked what the owner of the surface received in payment from a claimant who staked out a claim on it for the purpose of prosecuting mining and his answer was, "Nothing at all . . . . The mining customs do not recognize the surface land at all; the mining laws recognize the veins so far as the grantor goes, but every man has as much room as is necessary for dressing (treating ore) in the field."[44]

The barmaster of the High Peak when asked how far underground a miner might go as distinguished from the surface he required, answered, "he can go underground as far as he likes. Q. Can he drive his lode as far as he likes? Yes."[45] The Derbyshire extralateral right is the purest form of this right that exists. A certain length of vein is laid out on the surface and the miner has the right to follow this vein to unlimited depth between vertical planes passed through the ends of the claim at right angles to the course of the vein.[46] The vein was the principal thing and the surface an incident. In this respect, our Act of 1866 closely resembles the Derbyshire right.[47]

There has been considerable speculation as to the origin of the

---

[42] Houghton, Compleat Miner, pp. 94-101; Hardy, Miner's Guide (1749), pp. 142-150. As already noted, this is the same measure of the extralateral right that has been generally adopted in Germany and also in the United States under the Act of 1866, where in both cases the law was silent as to how this right should be measured.

[43] In Germany the "Bergmeister" and in early mining in France the "bourgmestres" performed similar functions.

[44] Third Report of the Royal Commission on Mining Royalties, p. 52.

[45] Id., p. 54.

[46] The Derbyshire rake-veins to which this measure was applied were, comparatively speaking, ideal veins, being nearly perpendicular, their hade or inclination being only one foot in ten and their course generally following a straight line. Mineralogy of Derbyshire, Mawe, pp. 32-33. Treatise on Ore Deposits, von Cotta (Trans. by Prime, p. 431.) The flat-veins of Derbyshire were taken up by claims 14 yards square. Houghton p. 2.

[47] The writer is the fortunate possessor of a rare work a'so edited by Houghton (1694) entitled "Articles to Establish and Confirm Laws, Liberties, & Customs of Silver & Gold Mines. . . . . in America . . . ." in which Houghton proposes that Parliament make mining laws substantially similar to those of Derbyshire applicable to the English colonies in Africa and America. In view of the strikingly similar miners' customs which eventually sprang up in the Western United

Derbyshire extralateral right. Hoover[48] believes that the law of this district is of Saxon importation. Blavier[49] says that the bye-laws of Derbyshire resemble the mining laws of Saxony. Smirke[50] states that many of the mining terms of ordinary use in Derbyshire correspond almost exactly with the *Platt Deutsch* terms of the German mines and that there is no difficulty in accounting for this when authentic records indicate the frequent importation into England and employment of German miners from 1271 down to the 18th century.[51] This view seems quite reasonable though Lewis in his work on the Stannaries intimates that the laws of the Derbyshire lead miners are customs dating back to a time beyond the memory of man and notes that Pliny refers to the fact that the lead miners in the interior of Britain are governed by certain rules of their own making.[52] This would antedate even Germanic influence. There is no question but that the Germanic impress is pronounced. That the extralateral right was an importation is doubtful, for if lead mining and customs dated back to the days of the Romans the exercise of that right had probably already taken place. It is the normal and natural way of mining on veins as steep in dip and as ideal in occurrence as are the rake veins of Derbyshire. The early miners with simple methods would pay little attention to surface rights which were comparatively value-less, except such limited portions as were required for their mining operations, and would merely stake out lengths of apex on the surface. There is no resemblance between the extralateral right of Saxony with its artificial planes in the hanging and foot walls of the vein accompanying it on the dip down into infinite depth and with a right to everything found between these planes, and the Derbyshire right to follow the vein only, subject to the condition that if the vein branched and the separation continued for the distance of half a meer, the branches were pronounced as two distinct veins. So long as the Rither,[53] or strip of country rock lying

---

States upon the discovery of Gold in 1848 this proposal is little short of prophetic.

[48] Hoover's Translation of Agricola, note p. 77.

[49] Jurisprudence des Mines, Vol. 1, p. 18.

[50] Stannaries of Cornwall (1843) p. 94 note g.

[51] See also Mander's Glossary of Technical Terms of Derbyshire Miners (1824) which notes a large number of words of Saxon and Teutonic origin and Raymond, Mineral Resources 1883-4, p. 996.

[52] The Stannaries (1908) pp. 82-83.

[53] The Saxon influence is seen even here for the word Rither is derived from the Saxon word "wrythan." Mander's Glossary, p. 60.

between the two veins "may be taken down by firing on the side, it is to be taken and reputed but for one vein, but in case the Rither be so thick that it cannot be taken by firing on the one side, and the Veins go so asunder, for half a Meer in length, then they are serviceable to the Miner, as two distinct Veins," and each was required to be taken up in a separate claim.[54] The fact that in both Derbyshire and Germany the longitudinal or end limits of the extralateral right in depth were vertical planes at right angles to the general course of the vein might support the view of common origin were it not for the fact that this is the natural and obvious limit and that no other mode of measurement is logical under the circumstances unless we invoke the parallel end line measurement of our federal act of 1872.

The lead miners in the forest of Mendip also mined under old customs which were not as complete in detail as the Derbyshire laws but similar in many respects and undoubtedly contemplating extralateral rights. The extent of the miner's or grovier's right to mine on the vein was ascertained by his standing "to the girdle or waste" in his groof or mine working and heaving his "hacke" or pickaxe "two ways after the rake" or vein. In modern language the miner stood waist deep in his discovery shaft and threw his pickaxe in each direction along the apex of the vein both forward and backward "as the chyne or rake goeth." This determined the extent of his boundaries.[55]

The lead deposits of Alston Moor were also another center of free mining with "liberties and Customs" similar in some respects to those just noted.[56]

In the famous Forest of Dean only male persons born in the hundred of St. Briavels and who had worked a year and a day in

---

[54] Houghton, Article XXXIV, p. 37.

[55] Smirke in his work on the Stannaries, p. 127, note c, makes the comment that this is a curious instance of the "Hammerwurf" of Teutonic antiquity and (p. 128, note e) has its parallel in the arrow flight of the Bohemian "montani" and in numerous instances cited by Grimm, Alterthümer, etc. In the Dean Forest (p. 132) "the pit (mine working) shall have such liberty and franchises that no man shall come within so much space the miner may stand and cast so far from him redding (ridding?) and stones with a bale, as the manner is; and shall have his marks pertaining to the said pit." The Laws and Orders of the Mendip Miners, commonly called Lord Choke's Laws are also found in a work on the County of Somerset by Billingsby (1797)) p. 23 seq.

[56] Lewis, pp. 79-80; Smirke pp. 124-5; The Mining Districts of Alston Moor (1833), Sopwith, p. 19.

a coal or iron mine were Free Miners and entitled to take up or "gale" these mines in the forest.[57] These Free Miners met at the "Speech House" and regulated the operation of their own laws and customs. In galing or granting the right to mine the gaveller (mine official) fixed a starting point and no other limit was assigned. No gale could be granted to another within 100 yards of this starting point. This distance was later increased till it reached 1000 yards. Since contiguous claims had no definite boundaries it became a matter of contention, or a "race of diligence" as our federal court has expressed a similar situation here, as to which miner could first obtain possession of the intervening ground by extending his workings.[58] These workings might be carried to an indefinite extent—"as far as the vein extends"—unless interrupted by another working.[59] Because of this great uncertainty as to ownership Parliament intervened and a Commission was appointed in 1838 which awarded definite boundaries to all legitimate claimants, and followed the ancient customs as far as possible, confining a claimant to one vein or bed and "underlying or other veins not so awarded or galed may be galed to other parties."[60]

Spain and Spanish America (Peru and Mexico). The fabulous wealth of the mines worked under Spanish rule, particularly in her possessions in the New World, stimulates our interest in her mining laws.

While we would naturally expect Spanish laws to reflect the influence of the civil law, we find little impress on her mining code from this source. In making an analytical study of the Spanish mining laws one is struck by the similarity of many of the provisions to those of the early Germanic mining codes, especially the

---

[57] Dean Forest Award, Sopwith (1841); Laws of Dean Forest, Wood (1878).

[58] "When parties under different gales were approaching each other, they might proceed until their mattocks should meet." Fourth Report, Dean Forest Commissioners, p. 8.

[59] Early Germanic mining claims were also unmeasured areas, the only regulation being one which forbade too close an approach to a neighboring claim, Lewis, 163 note 4.

[60] Sopwith, 167, 202. Free Miners also worked quarries of stone in the Forest of Dean, the lines of each gale or claim being parallel and at right angles from that side of the hill where the work first commenced. The Miner could not work laterally outside of those boundaries "but he may depart from the original horizontal line to suit the dip of the stone. The application of these rules is termed squaring the hill." Fifth Report of Dean Forest Commissioners, p. 73.

right of free mining, i. e., the right of the individual to go upon crown lands or even lands belonging to others and upon making a discovery of mineral becoming entitled as a matter of right to the possession of a mining claim including the discovery. But the similarity is accounted for when we learn that in framing the mining ordinances of Spain "recourse was had to the laws of Germany."[61]

Article 5 of the Spanish mining ordinances of 1559 referred to by Gamboa as the "old ordinances," provides that,

> "Whereas, by not designating the limit and space which the Mines that shall thus be discovered are to have, there may result great confusion, differences and lawsuits; and the first discoverer may pretend that his Mine and the right which by discovery may belong to him, cover and include the whole extent and continuation of the metallic vein, and that in the whole of such extent and continuation no person can interfere to prospect, search or work, from which may result great embarrassment and inpediment to the discovery, and working and development of said Mines,"

therefore, the article provides, the Mine or *pertenencia to* which a discoverer is entitled shall have definite surface boundaries, viz: 100 *varas* long and 50 *varas* wide.[62]

This provision would seem to have eliminated the exercise of any extralateral right and this is further borne out by Article 29 which provided that if Mines are staked out on the sides of another mine whose boundaries are already defined, because it appears that the vein inclines from the latter and may enter these side claims, the Court shall protect these side claimants and shall not permit the person who owns the mine from which the ore inclines, to follow the vein into these adjoining claims.

However, Article 30 also provided that if the boundaries of the mine from which the ore inclines are not already defined by the official survey and staking or if the ground into which the ore dips is not already claimed, then in either case the owner of the mine "shall be at liberty to continue to follow the said ore although

---

[61] Comentarios a las Ordenanzas de Minas, Gamboa (1759), p. 6; See also Heathfield's translation (1830) p. 8. These Commentaries by Gamboa constitute the classic work on mining law in Spanish. See also Smirke, Stannaries of Cornwall, p. 84 note z, where he states that, "The German system of jurisprudence on the subject of mines has met with general acceptance throughout the Continent of Europe, having been adopted in Russia; in the countries around the Baltic; in Spain; and in the extensive settlements of the latter country in America."

[62] Mining Laws of Spain & Mexico, Halleck (1859), p. 13.

he may go outside of his *pertenencia.*"[63] This latter provision clearly recognizes a limited exercise of the extralateral pursuit.[64]

Ordinance XXX of the Spanish Mining Code of 1584, referred to by Gamboa as the "new ordinances", provided that if the ore in any mine shall be continuous with the ore of any other mine "and the two mines shall become one, in the depth; the miner who shall have first sunk and made his way into the other mine," shall be entitled to the ore until the owner of the adjoining mine compels him to establish his boundaries. If it is found that he is outside of his true boundaries he must withdraw, but he is still entitled to the ore he has mined from the other's *pertenencia,* "inasmuch as he has acquired a right to it by the care and diligence used in working with more activity than his neighbor." The ordinance also provided that if a person took a *pertenencia* contiguous to the mine of another and there is no vein disclosed therein or if there is one and it contains no ore, but the claimant works "merely with the intention of profiting by the ore of his neighbor when he shall get within his boundaries" he acquires no rights "even though his neighbor's ore should take its course within his *pertenencia;* and our mining judges and justices shall determine it so, and shall not allow or permit such mines, not being upon a vein or ore, to be worked."[65] It is quite evident that the foregoing provisions create and protect a modified form of extralateral pursuit.

Gamboa comments that "Of all the ordinances contained in the new code, or the old law, there are none more difficult, or which have been more frequently the subject of litigation in the courts than this."[66] He states that when the vein extends outside the *pertenencias* of adjoining owners into unclaimed ground, each owner is entitled to work freely through the virgin ground upon the dip of the vein beyond his own limits and whenever the workings of rival claimants in this common ground meet a *guarda-raya* or boundary monument should be established beyond which neither could pass.[67] Cases of this character gave rise to extensive litigation and a famous contest arose in the mining district of Guan-

---

[63] Halleck, pp. 29-30.
[64] See, Heathfield's Gamboa, pp. 17-43.
[65] Heathfield's Gamboa. pp. 14-15.
[66] Id. pp. 17-18.
[67] Id. p. 25. Gamboa notes that this provision of the new ordinance repeals the policy of the old ordinance of confining a miner to his own boundaries but that this new provision is based on the desire of the sovereign to increase the amount of his royalties and also to reward industry and diligence. pp. 31-32.

axuato where Count de San Pedro del Alamo insisted that the underlay (dip) of the vein which apexed in his Santa Anita mine "was infinite in extent", that "the vein was his property, as far as it extended upon the underlay as being one and the same vein: and that as, when the vein, being what is called a deep vein, proceeds perpendicularly downward, the miner may work on to the antipodes, or to the infernal regions, as Amaya says; so, if the vein be inclined, its whole extent upon the underlay is granted to the miner."

The proprietors of an adjoining mine who had first occupied the vein in dispute outside their boundaries in common ground, insisted that the ordinances contemplated such mining and that boundary marks were to be erected underground wherever their workings met. This latter view was upheld by a decree of the royal *audiencia* in 1749.

The miners of this district had previously contended that the surface limits alone were to be within prescribed boundaries but insisted that the miner might work to an unlimited extent underground, whereupon in 1739 an order was issued that the property of the vein is not granted to an indefinite extent on the underlay and that the underground limits of the mine must correspond vertically with the surface boundaries. The only exception is that already noted which permits a miner to follow a vein into unclaimed ground.[68]

The early Spanish mining laws applicable to Peru provided that "if the principal vein of a mine should take its course without another's limits, it may be followed up without any impediment." If a vein divided before taking its course within the boundaries of a neighboring mine, the owner was required to select one of the branches as his principal vein which he could follow into his neighbor's ground. Gamboa notes that these regulations conform to the practice in the mines of Germany.[69]

The ordinance of 1783 materially changed the Spanish mining law.[70] Article I of Title VIII states that uniformity of size of surface claims cannot be observed underground and at the same time equality between claimants preserved, for the inclination of the vein with the plane of the horizon makes the amount of vein

[68] Id. pp. 26-31.
[69] Id., pp. 42-43. See also, Gazophilatium Regium Perubicum, Escalona (1675) Lib. II, Part II, Cap. I.
[70] These ordinances are set forth in full in Halleck's Mining Laws of Spain & Mexico, pp. 189-315.

material included within the *pertenencia* greater or smaller and it may well happen that when a miner after great expense and labor, reaches the boundaries of his claim where the vein begins to be rich, an adjoining owner, who has placed himself at that point with more cunning than labor, may compel him to stop working further "so that from this arises one of the greatest and most frequent causes of litigation and dissension among miners."[71] As a result, the new code provided that each miner is entitled to 200 Castillian *varas* which are called *de medir* (long or running measure) along the thread, direction or course of the vein taken on a level. To square the claim a rectangle was formed by taking 100 *varas* on each or either side of the vein, if the vein were vertical, and this width increased as the dip of the vein might flatten till the claim attained a maximum width of 200 *varas* for veins dipping at an angle of 45° or less. The ordinances voiced the opinion that by the time the vertical boundaries of the claim were reached the vein will have been considerably exhausted.

Article 14 referring to the permission granted under the former law of 1584 to enter another mine and continue following the vein until the owner of the other mine can extend his workings so as to stop the adverse entry, states that it is "the most fruitful cause of the bitterest law suits, dissensions and disturbances among miners" and the adverse entry occurs more often through fraud or accident rather than as the result of merit or industry. Therefore, entering the *pertenencia* of another is prohibited.

Article 15 provides for an exception, however, and if a miner pursuing his working fairly and following his vein reaches the *pertenencia* of another or discovers there a vein undiscovered by the adjoining owner, he shall be obliged to give such adjoining owner immediate notice and thereafter share equally with him all that he may extract from the adjoining *pertenencia* and for failure to give such notice of invasion of the other's territory he lost all right to the ore taken out and also paid double its value as a penalty. The other owner could stop this invasion at any point that his own workings encountered the invader's.

Article 16 continued the right to follow the vein into unclaimed

---

[71] In the light of the present day criticism of the extralateral right, it is amusing to note that this ordinance attributes excessive litigation to the inflexible vertical boundary system. Dissatisfaction with existing conditions and enthusiastic conviction that a change will result in complete relief, is a common characteristic which is not confined to the present day.

adjoining territory but compelled the denouncing of a new adjoining *pertenencia* covering the vein.

Article 17 confirmed each owner to that portion of the vein included within his boundaries and specifically denied the right either to the discoverer of the vein or to the owner of the apex to "claim it in its whole extent, or wherever it may happen to be."

This was the mining law in force in Mexico from 1783 up to the time of the discovery of gold in California. Raymond[72] makes the comment that

> "this law is remarkable for an attempt to reconcile the two systems of square and inclined locations by an elaborate graduation of the size and shape of the surface claim according to the dip of the vein."

He points out the impossibility of administering such a law in accordance with the facts, for an opening 10 yards deep was required to determine the dip of the vein which was then erroneously assumed to follow a uniform course and dip.[73]

The ordinances of 1783 have long since been superseded by mining codes which have abolished the graduated forms of claims.

Italy (Neapolitan States). Article 15 of the Act of 1826 permits the worker of a mine which has been opened on one property to follow it into an adjoining property without the owner of the latter being able to prevent him; but in this case the latter has a right to be compensated, such compensation to be mutually agreed on or fixed by the arbitration of a judge. Apparently this right was only applicable to mines worked under private grants.[74]

Belgium. The mining laws of Belgium are based on the French code. In Liège adventurers appear to have had rights under certain circumstances of following seams and beds.[75]

Australia. The local court regulations of Maldon of March 6, 1857, provided that the width of a claim should be 100 feet on each side of the line of the reef with the dips and angles of all reefs

---

[72] Mineral Resources (1869), p. 196.

[73] Id., p. 198.

[74] Walmesley, Mining Laws of the World (1894) p. 106. The author makes the comment that this "right seems to be analogous to that which is recognized by the law of the United States of America." The mining laws of the various states of which Italy is composed vary materially, so each must be studied by itself. In Piedmont the resemblance to the mining law of France is marked, while the Austro-Hungarian influence, which is essentially Germanic in character, is evident in Venetia. Walmesley, pp. 95, 109.

[75] Walmesley, p. 120. See also De Fooz.

within the boundary and the right to follow them to whatever distance they might dip.[76]

In New South Wales the mining regulations of August 5, 1858, provided that:

> "Miners occupying any portion of a quartz reef or vein shall be entitled to follow and work it in any direction that such reef or vein may take. . . . . Provided . . . . that when any reef, vein or bed of quartz shall lie nearly horizontal, or at a less angle with the horizon than 20°,[77] the holder of any claim shall be only entitled to follow such reef, vein, or bed of quartz in the direction of the dip, for a distance not exceeding 50 yards from the point where they commence to sink in search of any such reef, vein, or bed of quartz."[78]

These extralateral provisions were probably patterned after the miners' customs of California, since California miners are known to have taken a leading part in this early mining in Australia. The use of the terms "dip and angles" is similar to language employed here by the early miners. Where the vein was inclined, the limits of a claim were determined by establishing a base line passed through the "peg" or discovery point on the apex of the vein and "another point visible and as distant as possible on the known line of the reef" or in case the position of the reef (vein) was not sufficiently known, an arbitrary point was selected and from this base line right angled lines were extended out in the direction of the dip of the vein. This method of defining boundaries within which the miner could work is almost identical with the plan which was later adopted on the Comstock lode for the settlement of disputes over boundaries.[79]

In 1862 the regulations were altered so that a claim had a width of 100 yards and the owner was entitled to all veins found therein,

---

[76] Law of Gold Mining in Australia and New Zealand, Armstrong (1901).

[77] If this provision was not suggested by the Germanic extra-lateral law, it is at least the strongest kind of circumstantial evidence, for in most of the mining districts of Germany veins that dipped at an angle of less than 20° were termed Flötze and no extralateral right could be acquired to such deposits.

[78] See, Mining Laws of Australia and New Zealand, Veatch (1910).

[79] A very interesting volume entitled, "The Law of the Apex," by Kenny has recently appeared, (1914), in which the author advocates the adoption of a similar plan of measurement in the United States in place of the present system of parallel end lines under the Act of 1872. There is considerable reason underlying the suggestion, for it doubtless affords a more logical division of the vein than any other system which could be devised, but the conception is based on ideal vein conditions and does not take into consideration geological complexities.

instead of one vein only as under the former act, and could follow any reef into unoccupied ground.[80] In 1866 the system of vertical boundaries was adopted because the extralateral system was "found to lead to disputes."

In other parts of Australia the locator along the apex of the vein had a preferential right to acquire "frontage claims" overlying the dip. This is analogous to the extension of the mine perimeter in the direction of the dip under the French law.

In Western Australia under existing law, individual leases are granted of areas necessary to work the reef to a depth of 3000 feet and if the mineral is gold the length along the outcrop of the reef shall not exceed 66 chains, and if mineral other than gold the distance along the outcrop shall not exceed 90 chains. This right to mine in depth is virtually equivalent to the exercise of an extralateral right.

Rhodesia. All property in minerals and mining rights in Rhodesia has been granted by the Crown to the British South Africa Company. The system of mining law in force there was adopted in 1903 and is largely copied from the American law.[81] A "reef claim" is a parallelogram 150 feet in length along the course of the reef with a width of 600 feet at right angles to the length. A "block" is a group of not to exceed ten contiguous reef claims thus forming a parallelogram 1500 by 600 feet, the exact size of a lode claim under American law. The "extralateral right" is defined in the ordinance to be "the right of following a reef on its dip in any block beyond the limits of the vertical block." The "course of a reef" is defined to be a line on the surface marking the intersection of the center of the reef with such surface. If the reef were "blind," i. e., situated below the surface the points where it approached closest to the surface were projected vertically upward. This is the "course of the apex" or "lode line" of the American law.

The miner had the

> "extralateral right of pursuit of such portions of his discovery reef on its dip outside the limits of his vertical block as are comprised between vertical planes indefinitely extended and passing through the end lines of his block."[82]

Canada (British Columbia). The various provinces of Canada have adopted the vertical boundary system of mining law but

---

[80] Here we have a provision similar to those contained in the Spanish Mining Codes already noted.

[81] Mining Law of the British Empire, Alford (1906), p. 197.

[82] The striking similarity of this law to the American Mining Law is evident. The trial of the first important case involving the extra-

British Columbia in 1891 passed a mineral act, section 31 of which provided that:

> "The lawful holders of mineral claims shall have the exclusive right of possession of all the surface included within the lines of their locations, and of all veins, lodes and ledges throughout their entire depth, the top or apex of which lies inside of such surface lines extended downward vertically, although such veins, lodes or ledges may so far depart from a perpendicular in their course downward as to extend outside the vertical side lines of such surface locations," etc.[83]

The section also provided that if a location were laid crosswise of a vein instead of along its course the locator secured only so much of the vein or lode as it crossed and the side lines became the end lines for the purpose of defining extralateral rights. A location was deemed to be laid crosswise when the angle made by the center line of the location and the general course of the vein was greater than 45 degrees.

This section of the Act was repealed by Section 2 of the Amendment Act of 1892 which provided,[84] that "The owner of a mineral claim shall be entitled to all minerals which may lie within his claim, but he shall not be entitled to mine outside the boundary lines of his claim continued vertically downward." Subsection b, preserves rights of locations under the former acts.[85]

As a result of this brief period during which the extralateral right was sanctioned, rights to a number of such mining claims became vested. The British Columbia reports indicate that several cases have arisen where these rights are involved.

Central and South America. Many of these countries, notably Uruguay, Venezuela, Nicaragua, and Honduras, have features copied from the Spanish law, either permitting a claimant to mine on the vein into the subsurface of his neighbor and accounting to the latter for one half of the net proceeds of all ore extracted

---

lateral right feature of Rhodesian mining law to be brought to England was recently concluded in London. The Amalgamated Properties of Rhodesia brought suit against the Globe & Phoenix Gold Mining Company Ltd. for the recovery of approximately $1,000,000, alleged to have been wrongfully extracted from the John Bull claims. The case turned largely on geological facts and the usual array of expert talent characteristic of such cases was present. The writer is indebted to Mr. H. W. Turner for the clippings of the London papers reporting the proceedings.

[83] This is identical in language with the Act of 1872, § 2322 U. S. Rev. Stats., from which it was unquestionably taken. The writer is informed that British Columbia first adopted the extralateral right in 1882.

[84] §15, subd. a.

[85] Centre Star Mining Company v. Iron Mask Mining Company (1898), 6 British Columbia Cases, 355; Martin, Min. Cases 267 note, and pp. 629-630, 681-682.

but subject to being stopped from further working whenever the neighbor reaches the trespass workings, or permitting a claimant to enter the subsurface of abandoned or unclaimed subsurface with the right to denounce an adjoining claim in such direction.

Of greater interest are the Mining Regulations of British Guiana of 1887 which give the right to follow veins throughout their entire depth where the apex is included within the surface boundaries of the claim but the right of such outside pursuit is confined between vertical end line planes. There was an additional privilege putting a premium on the one who first commences working on the vein extralaterally. Our federal mining Act of 1872 is clearly responsible for the main extralateral feature.[85a]

There are doubtless other parts of the world where the extralateral right or some modification of it has at some time been exercised.[86]

The attempt has been made to include in this article all the examples of the exercise of such a right that have come to the writer's attention. In many of the other countries such as China, Russia, etc., it has been quite customary to secure a concession to a mine which includes the entire vein and there would be no necessity for adjusting rights between adjoining owners. Sufficient examples have been presented to indicate that there has been ·a powerful tendency at work based on fundamental reason and natural law to segregate the mineral bearing vein from the surface, and to grant the vein to the miner. Instead of confining him to inflexible surface boundaries extended downward vertically, the tendency has been to make these boundaries more elastic so that he could, in the interest of economy and justice, follow down on his vein, which is the principal thing sought, and which has no logical relation to the overlying surface. The surface ownership was usually segregated from the underlying mineral and vested in another who might be devoting it to agricultural or other pursuits. This severance is in line with the highest economic use of natural resources and embodies the modern conception of conservation. The surface was frequently uséd for convenience in marking out a perimeter merely to place a limit on underground workings, but the perimeter

---

[85a] "Mines and Mining Laws of Latin America, published by the Bureau of the American Republics, April 1892.

[86] Mr. Horace V. Winchell mentions Sweden as one of the countries where the extralateral right was operative for a time. Report of Meeting of the Mining & Metallurgical Society of America, December 1915. Reprint, Senate Document No. 233, 64th Congress 1st Session, p. 57.

could be varied or extended according to the nature of the deposit, and as underground development might indicate was most equitable and economic. Frontage claims also accomplished the same object.

The pure type of extralateral right has unquestionably given rise to a vast amount of litigation, and this fact has resulted in its abolition in most countries where it formerly existed.

In a subsequent article the writer plans to trace the growth and operation of the extralateral right in the United States and to call attention to some serious problems which must be solved in the event that it is abolished. *Wm. E. Colby.*
Berkeley, California.

Volume IV.   SEPTEMBER, 1916   Number 6

II. The Origin and Development of the Extralateral Right in the United States.

THE discovery of gold in California in January of 1848, brought about the birth of a distinctive American mining law. Theretofore, no general mining law was in force in the United States and the few Acts of Congress on the subject were local in character, applying only to the lead and copper deposits of the Middle West, and were not based on any well defined policy. The general tendency was to place mineral lands on the same basis as agricultural lands.[1] There was no trace of any exercise of an extralateral right to be found in any of these early laws.

The news of the finding of the fabulous gold fields of California spread around the world like wildfire and miners from every part of the globe flocked to the new Eldorado to share in its treasure. Miners came from the lead mines of Illinois and Wisconsin, from the copper mines of Michigan, from the gold mines of Virginia, Georgia and the Carolinas, from the tin mines of Cornwall, the lead mines of Derbyshire, the silver and copper mines of Germany, the silver and gold mines of Mexico and Peru, and in fact from every known mining community. They brought their varied experience and were joined by countless others who had no previous mining experience of any sort.[2] It must be borne in mind that no general mining law was in force in this new territory. Colonel Mason, the military governor of California in 1848, issued

---

[1] Those who are interested in the early history of mining law in the United States will find an excellent presentation in Lindley on Mines, (3rd ed.), §§ 28-36. See also Donaldson, The Public Domain (1883), pp. 306-309.

[2] The fascinating history of the days of '49 is outlined in Lindley on Mines, (3rd ed.) chapter 3, §§ 40-40, and Crane, Treatise on Gold and Silver, pp. 54-62. Also see Browne, Mineral Resources, 1867, pp. 15-16, 38.

a proclamation abolishing "the Mexican laws and customs now prevailing in California relative to the denouncement of mines."[3] His action was unnecessary, however, since the Supreme Court of the United States later held[4] that the Mexican law relating to the acquisition of mining property was not operative in California because of the absence of any mining officials required by the Mexican law.

This situation is important to bear in mind, for one would naturally suppose that the mining laws which developed in this territory would have borne the distinct impress of the Mexican and Spanish mining laws which were, theoretically, at least, in force throughout the greater part of the West while it remained under the sovereignty of Mexico. As a matter of fact, with the exception of a small amount of placer mining for gold in the vicinity of Los Angeles[5] and mining for quicksilver at New Almaden,[6] Santa Clara County, there was no mining of any noteworthy character being carried on in this vast and largely unexplored domain. This accounts for the absence of Mexican mining deputations with whom mining claims were required to be registered under Mexican law.

With the Mexican law of mines inoperative, with no existing congressional legislation on mines applicable, with state government in the West either non-existent or in its infancy, the field was open for the adoption of that form of mining law which might best fit the new conditions. As already noted, there had been no federal mining law of any consequence in the older portions of the United States which might serve as a pattern. The common law of England which was in force in most of the Eastern states had little bearing on mining problems. As a consequence, those who came from other parts of the United States, and who constituted the major part of the army of gold seekers,[7] and even those who had previous experience in the mines of the Middle West and Georgia, brought with them little knowledge of a suitable mining

---

[3] Yale, Mining Claims (1867), p. 17.

[4] United States v. Castellero (1862), 67 U. S. 17-371, 17 L. Ed. 360.

[5] Browne, Mineral Resources (1867), pp. 13-14, 38; Crane, Gold and Silver, p. 54.

[6] United States v. Castellero, supra, n. 4.

[7] Josiah Royce says "The effective majority in all the chief communities was formed of Americans. . . ." Royce, California, p. 225. They were "educated, intelligent, civilized and elevated men of the best classes of society." California Herald (New York) Jan. 16, 1849.

code. There were, however, thrown into this melting pot of nations, foreigners who arrived with a knowledge of the mining laws in force in other parts of the world. Germans, Cornishmen, Mexicans, Peruvians, came from countries in which complete mining codes were operative. It would be strange indeed if these experienced miners did not take an active part in the councils which followed and to some degree, at least, influence the shaping of the laws which emerged from this chaotic condition.

Going out into the wild and uninhabited mountains and cañons of the Sierras, these pioneers found no laws in force or which could be made applicable to the new conditions they had to meet. The necessities of the situation and the absence of any effective sovereign authority to impose laws and enforce obedience on this army of gold seekers, who suddenly overran the rugged slopes of the Sierras like a swarm of ants, brought about one of the most remarkable and purely democratic governmental institutions in the history of the world. Wherever there was a mining center of any importance a meeting was called and the miners of the vicinity assembled, organized a mining district, elected officers and adopted a brief and usually rather crude code of laws by which the district was to be governed. These district rules and regulations constituted the miners' laws and customs [8] and were mainly devoted to the regulation of mining, though in the early days before the State had assumed the effective administration of justice, these laws frequently dealt with other civil rights and the punishment of crimes.[9]

---

[8] "A special kind of law, a sort of common law of the miners, the offspring of a nation's irrepressible march,—lawless in some senses, yet clothed with dignity by a conception of the immense social results mingled with the fortunes of these bold investigators,—has sprung up on the Pacific Coast, and presents in the value of a 'mining right' a novel and peculiar question of jurisdiction for this Court." Sparrow v. Strong (1865), 70 U. S. 97, 18 L. Ed. 49.

[9] The following extracts are taken from editorials of the Evening Picayune of San Francisco:

"The rules by which the rights of discoverers are defined and protected among those concerned in mining operations, have thus far, we believe, been as much respected as legislative enactments would be. (December 11, 1850).

"The fact was, and still is, in respect to the great mass of American citizens engaged in practical mining, that they have very little care for the creation, support, or character of any government in the State. The rules of their mutual adoption, by which their rights of property are protected, answer quite well the purposes for which they would desire any legislation, and their own mode of securing justice under those rules, is probably more instant and certain than such as would be prescribed by

It would be out of place here to discuss in detail the nature of these interesting rules.[10]

For present purposes it is sufficient to quote the following classic and concise statement of the situation by the Supreme Court of the United States speaking through Justice Field:[11]

"The discovery of gold in California was followed, as is well known, by an immense immigration into the State, which increased its population within three or four years from a few thousand to several hundred thousand. The lands in which the precious metals were found belonged to the United States, and were unsurveyed, and not open, by law, to occupation and settlement. Little was known of them further than that they were situated in the Sierra Nevada mountains. Into these mountains the emigrants in vast numbers penetrated, occupying the ravines, gulches and cañons, and probing the earth in all directions for the precious metals. Wherever they went, they carried with them that love of order and system and of fair dealing which are the prominent characteristics of our people. In every district which they occupied they framed certain rules for their government, by which the extent of ground they could severally hold for mining was designated, their possessory right to such ground secured and enforced, and contests between them either avoided or determined. These rules bore a marked similarity, varying in the several districts only according to the extent and character of the mines; distinct provisions being made for different kinds of mining, such as placer mining, quartz mining, and mining in drifts or tunnels. They all recognized discovery, followed by appropriation, as the foundation of the possessor's title, and development by working as the condition of its retention. And they were so framed as to secure to all comers, within practicable limits, absolute equality of right and privilege in working the mines. Nothing but such equality would have been

---

laws of the legislature. . . ." (December 14, 1850).

". . . for the present we know of no class of people who are better able to regulate the disposition of the mineral lands of California than the miners themselves, at any rate they have done very well so far." (January 31, 1851).

[10] Those who are interested in the subject will find these miner's laws elaborately treated in Lindley on Mines, Chapter 3; Browne, Mineral Resources, (1867), pp. 226-264; Yale, Title to Mining Claims, etc., (1867), pp. 58-88; Bancroft's Handbook of Mining (1861), pp. 189-203; Morton v. Solambo M. Co. (1864), 26 Cal. 527, 532-533; Shinn, Mining Camps (1885); Royce, California (1886). A veritable mine of original information is to be found in Vol. XIV of the Tenth U. S. Census (1885), which gives in full the miner's rules of most of the districts of the West. This invaluable compilation was made through the wise foresight of Clarence King, who was prominently identified with the mining industry.

[11] Jennison v. Kirk (1878), 98 U. S. 453, 457-458, 25 L. Ed. 240.

tolerated by the miners, who were emphatically the law-makers, as respects mining, upon the public lands in the State. The first appropriator was everywhere held to have, within certain well-defined limits, a better right than others to the claims taken up; and in all controversies, except as against the government, he was regarded as the original owner, from whom title was to be traced."

The Supreme Court of California had earlier commented on this unique condition, saying: [12]

"Courts are bound to take notice of the political and social condition of the country, which they judicially rule. In this State the larger part of the territory consists of mineral lands, nearly the whole of which are the property of the public. No right or intent of disposition of these lands has been shown either by the United States or the State governments, and with the exception of certain State regulations, very limited in their character, a system has been permitted to grow up by the voluntary action and assent of the population, whose free and unrestrained occupation of the mineral region has been tacitly assented to by the one government, and heartily encouraged by the expressed legislative policy of the other. If there are, as must be admitted, many things connected with this system, which are crude and undigested, and subject to fluctuation and dispute, there are still some which a universal sense of necessity and propriety have so firmly fixed as that they have come to be looked upon as having the force and effect of res judicata. Among these the most important are the rights of miners to be protected in the possession of their selected localities, and the rights of those who, by prior appropriation, have taken the waters from their natural beds, and by costly artificial works have conducted them for miles over mountains and ravines, to supply the necessities of gold diggers, and without which the most important interests of the mineral region would remain without development. So fully recognized have become these rights that without any specific legislation conferring or confirming them, they are alluded to and spoken of in various acts of the Legislature in the same manner as if they were rights which had been vested by the most distinct expression of the will of the law-makers. . . ."

The main objects of the regulations were to fix the boundaries of the districts, the size of the claims, the manner in which the claims were to be marked and recorded, the amount of work which was required to keep the title alive and the circumstances under

---

[12] Irwin v. Phillips (1855), 5 Cal. 140, 146.

which the claim was to be considered as abandoned or forfeited.[13]

As far as the regulation of mining was concerned they became "the law of the land." Their observance was general and the Legislature of the State of California recognized them as being of controlling effect in the absence of congressional or state action.[14]

Other Western states and territories also gave them similar recognition and the courts upheld them as being of controlling force.[15]

Water rights necessary for working placer claims also became a subject of considerable importance as the placer mining increased and many districts had rules governing the acquisition of these rights.[16]

The early mining, following the discovery of gold, was, for a considerable time, confined to the placers. There was an abundance of virgin ground and the gold in the form of dust or nuggets when separated from the gravels required no further treatment but became the medium of exchange and to a great extent took the place of coin. On the other hand, quartz mining involved the more difficult extraction of vein material and treatment of the ores when extracted. A quartz mine took time to develop in order to determine whether the quantity and grade of the ore available justified the great expense of erecting a mill. The mining regions were remote from centers of civilization and the lack of facilities for making mining machinery and the prohibitive cost of transporting it to the mines when made, also tended to delay quartz mining. This accounts for the fact that many months elapsed before it assumed any considerable importance.

---

[13] Browne, Mineral Resources (1867), p. 226; Yale, Mining Claims (1867), p. 61.

[14] Section 621 of the California Practice Act of 1851 provided that: "In actions respecting 'mining claims', proof shall be admitted of the customs, usages or regulations established and in force at the bar or diggings embracing such claims; and such customs, usages or regulations, when not in conflict with the Constitution and laws of this State, shall govern the decision of the action."

[15] "A series of wise judicial decisions moulded these regulations and customs into a comprehensive system of common law, embracing not only mining law (properly speaking), but also regulating the use of water for mining purposes. The same system has spread over all the interior states and territories where mines have been found, as far east as the Missouri river." (Remarks of Senator Stewart before the U. S. Senate, June 18, 1866). Appendix No. 1, 70 U. S. 778.

[16] See: Wiel, Water Rights in the Western States, §§ 66-91. The doctrine of prior appropriation as applied to water is not the unique creation of the miners of the West as many have supposed. This doctrine had

There is some difference of opinion as to when quartz mining began in California. There is no doubt but that in 1850 rich outcrops of gold-bearing quartz had been discovered and located.[17]

The Morgan Mine on Carson Hill in Calaveras County is reported to have been discovered in February, 1850, and over two million dollars taken out in a little over a year. The ore was so rich that much of it was treated in hand mortars. The remainder was ground in arrastras, as most of the miners employed by the owners were Mexicans and this was the old Spanish method of treating ore.[18]

In Mariposa County on the Jackson lode, fifteen Cornish miners were employed and a steam quartz mill was erected in September, 1850, having been purchased in San Francisco in May.[19]

"Highgrade" quartz showing free gold was found at Gold Hill near Grass Valley in Nevada County in October, 1850. Other discoveries were made immediately following this one. A quartz mill was erected at Grass Valley by two Germans during this same year.[20]

It is quite evident that quartz mining had become common by the end of 1850, and these reports of the earliest operations are particularly interesting to those seeking the source of our quartz mining laws, as indicating that Germanic, Cornish and Spanish influence were each intimately associated with this early quartz mining.

Following closely on the discovery of quartz veins which could

---

been in force in the mining districts of the Germanic states for centuries. The writer has collected considerable interesting material on this subject from original sources which he hopes to present at some future time.

[17] Browne, Mineral Resources (1867), p. 20.

[18] Browne, Mineral Resources (1868), p. 59. The ore in this mine near the outcrop was so fabulously rich that a band of ruffians under the leadership of Billy Mulligan drove the owners away by force and worked it themselves until ejected by Court. Cases involving this mine were appealed to the Supreme Court of the State on six different occasions and in none of these cases was the question of extralateral rights raised, indicating that there are other prolific sources of litigation. The first suit which is reported was brought upon a contract of limited partnership entered into March, 1850, in Alabama and which contemplated the erection of a quartz mill which appears to have been accomplished in the Fall of 1850 at Carson Hill in order to treat ores from the Morgan Mine. Ross v. Austill (1852), 2 Cal. 183. This mine was subsequently acquired by James G. Fair and is now owned by one of his heirs.

[19] Gregory Yale states in his work on "Titles to Mining Claims, Etc." (1867), that he was one of the victimized shareholders in this company p. 58, note.

[20] Crane, Gold and Silver, pp. 59, 122.

be profitably worked, we find that district rules and regulations were adopted governing their acquisition. The earliest set of rules of which we have any record was adopted December 30th, 1850, by the Gold Mountain Mining District, Nevada County, California. These provided that "thirty by forty feet shall constitute a full claim."[21] On February 30th, 1851, the neighboring Union Quartz Mountain Mining District adopted an identical provision and in May, 1851, claims sixty feet square were authorized on Kentucky Hill.[21a] These rules were doubtless patterned after placer district regulations which in many instances allotted a small, rectangular, superficial area to each claimant.[22] There was clearly no attempt to confer an extralateral right or right to follow a vein indefinitely on its downward course.[23]

The first appearance of the extralateral right in any district regulations that has come to the writer's attention is to be found in those adopted June 6th, 1851, in the Saunder's Ledge Mining District also situated in Nevada County. Article 3rd of these local laws states that "One hundred feet on the ledge *with the dips and angles* shall constitute a claim."[24] Here we have a typical grant of the right expressed in its simplest form. If there were only an opportunity to examine the miners who attended that meeting and ascertain the reason which prompted the selection of this form of measurement, the question as to the origin of our extralateral right might be easily solved. Did they have in mind the mining laws of Germany or Derbyshire, England, or merely the simple idea that the vein and not the surface ground was the thing of value which they were seeking to acquire a right to and that to divide it up into segments along its length was the only obvious way to apportion it? Probably this question will never be conclusively answered. The time has long since elapsed when any persons who took part in that meeting can be interviewed and

---

[21] Vol. XIV, Tenth U. S. Census (Mining Laws), p. 30.

[21a] Id. pp. 332-333.

[22] In his report of 1867 on Mineral Resources, p. 231, J. Ross Browne states that the early quartz regulations were framed "under the influence of persons familiar only with small claims customary in the placers."

[23] This is explained in part, at least, by Mr. Arthur Foote of Grass Valley who has informed the writer that the ledge on Gold Mountain where the earliest regulations were framed is flat lying and the exercise there of an extralateral right would be much less appropriate than on veins with a steeper dip.

[24] Vol. XIV, Tenth U. S. Census, p. 334.

unless some diary or other private records exist, of which there is no great likelihood at this late date, the matter will be left to speculation and conjecture.

Reasoning from the facts presented on the face of the provision itself, there is considerable circumstantial evidence to sustain the generally accepted view that the source of this regulation is to be found in the mining law of Derbyshire. The linear measurement of one hundred feet is practically the same as that of the Derbyshire claims which varied from twenty-seven to thirty-two yards in length.[25] The words "dips and angles" are old English terms such as would naturally be used in Derbyshire and the simple manner of marking off lengths along the ledge is peculiar to the Derbyshire extralateral right which is one of the purest and simplest forms of this right. On the other hand, we have ample evidence that German miners were already mining in this vicinity and that they had constructed a quartz mill at Grass Valley.[26]

If these miners from Germany were responsible for the adoption of the extralateral right in Saunder's Ledge Mining District, they could only have suggested the general idea, for the Germanic extralateral right was of an entirely different character, giving the right to mine between parallel planes [27] following the vein in depth on each side with all of its turnings and variations.[28]

---

[25] See: 4 California Law Review, 375.

[26] The writer has read many of the published diaries of "Forty-niners" and local newspapers of that period and finds ample evidence to support the statement that skilled miners from Germany were in California in considerable numbers by 1850. He possesses a curious little book entitled, "The German Emigrants or Voyage to California," published about 1851 in Germany which contains the following interesting statement: "In the Spring of the year 1851, there was an unusual stir and bustle in the village of Joachimsthal. [This is the famous silver mining district of the Middle Ages and our word "dollar" is derived from this valley or *Thal*, so intimately associated with silver.] The rage for emigration and a restless longing to try their luck beyond the seas, had attained a height bordering on frenzy. . . . The excitement was daily gaining ground to such an extent, that the agent of an American Emigration Company was welcomed and honored as a special messenger sent by Providence."

[27] Strictly speaking, these are not true planes since they conform to all of the rolls and curvatures of the vein. They are, properly speaking, surfaces, but the use of the latter term might lead to confusion with the surface of the ground.

[28] Though mining claims to which the extralateral rights attached were abolished in most of the Germanic States by the time of the gold rush to California, yet all vested rights were recognized and thousands of the oldest and best known mines in Germany were still entitled to, and did exercise this right, as many of them have continued to up to the present time. 4 California Law Review, 368-369.

It is a noteworthy coincidence that on June 7th, 1851, on the day following the Saunder's Ledge meeting, the quartz miners of Drytown Mining District, Amador County, "Resolved, 3rd: That the size of a claim in quartz veins shall be two hundred and forty (240) feet in length of the vein *without regard to the width* to the discoverer or company and one hundred and twenty (120) feet in addition thereto for each member of the company, etc." [29] On June 25th, 1851, or only nineteen days after the Saunder's Ledge rules were adopted, the miners of Mariposa County met at Quartzburg and framed a set of local laws which provided:

> "That all quartz veins now owned or occupied in the County of Mariposa, or which may be hereafter discovered or claimed, shall be governed by the following rules, to-wit: The interest of a party making a discovery of quartz shall be five hundred feet in length, and *the entire width of the vein, be that more or less.* The interests of all persons claiming subsequently to the discovery shall be two hundred and fifty feet in length, and the entire width of the vein." [30]

Here we have a distinct use of language to convey the same idea of an extralateral grant. The phrases "without regard to the width" and "the entire width of the vein, be that more or less," are clearly to remove any idea of lateral limitation from the prescribed linear measurement. Here again one might argue that the influence of the Derbyshire law is evident, for in Derbyshire the discoverer of any "new Rake or vein" was entitled to two "meers" or measures of length along the vein.[31] While both the Spanish-Mexican and Germanic laws rewarded the discoverer with additional ground, so that this feature of mining law had become quite universally accepted throughout the world, yet it was only in Derbyshire that two full claims were allowed him.

On October 1st, 1851, the Day's Ledge Mining District in Nevada County adopted by-laws, article first of which provided that "Claims shall be fifty feet along the course of the ledge, with its

---

[29] Vol. XIV, Tenth U. S. Census, p. 271. In adopting these resolutions "it was urged that fifty feet of a vein which probably had no bottom, was quite enough to satisfy any reasonable man." Gold-bearing quartz was first discovered in Amador Creek in February, 1851. A mill was erected but proved a failure till an experienced German miner came upon the scene. The historian says "the number of talented men in this convention was noted although it was not unusual for such bodies in the early fifties to be composed of men who might have sat in legislative halls with credit to themselves and all concerned." History of Amador County (1881), pp. 145-146.

[30] Id., p. 272.

[31] 4 California Law Review, 375.

dips, breadths, and angles."[32] Following in rapid succession in 1851, and particularly in 1852, and even as late as 1855, new mining districts were formed in Nevada County, most of which provided that claims should be one hundred feet along the ledge with the "dips and angles." Some of the regulations added the words "breadths," others "depths"[33] and it is particularly noteworthy that the Grass Valley Quartz Mining District regulations of December 20th, 1852, used the language "dips, angles and variations" of the vein,[34] which is the identical language later adopted by Congress in the first general mining act of 1866.[35] The regulations of Grizzly Flat Mining District of El Dorado County passed February 4th, 1852, provided that "One hundred and fifty feet in length and the dip or inclination of said lead to any depth and its width constitute one claim."[36] The use of the term "spurs" appears in the local rules of Angel's Mining District, Calaveras County, adopted July 20th, 1855, which granted one hundred feet on the length of a vein and, "all the dips, spurs or angles."[37] This also is of interest, for the Sutro Tunnel Act passed by Congress July 25th, 1866,[38] uses the terms "dips, spurs and angles" as applied to the veins that might be encountered by the tunnel and these terms were in common use in written conveyances of quartz claims.[39]

Other terms which are distinctly Cornish in origin and also in use in Derbyshire are found, such as "slides" meaning cross fissures,[40] "Fitters" which is undoubtedly a corruption of the Old Eng-

[32] Vol. XIV, Tenth U. S. Census, p. 334.

[33] Id. pp. 330-345.

[34] Id. p. 330.

[35] This language was carried by the Nevada County miners to the Comstock and vicinity and adopted by Senator Stewart in framing the Act of 1866.

[36] Id. p. 275. The word "lead" is an old English term from which the word "lode" was derived and both were in common use in Cornwall and to some extent in Derbyshire. (Bullion M. Co. v. Croesus M. Co. (1866), 2 Nev. 168, 176, says lode is "a Cornish word nearly synonomous with vein.") De la Beche says in his masterly work on the Geology of Cornwall, (1839), that lode "is a leading body traversing rocks" and "is a term employed in Cornwall and Devon for a mineral vein." (pp. 285 note, 343). The widespread use of this term in the early days of mining here establishes the influence of miners from England.

[37] Id. p. 285.

[38] 14 U. S. Stats. 242.

[39] As a matter of fact, the term "spurs" was in common use in the early days of quartz mining. The writer has a copy of a record of a location of the Morgan Mine on Carson Hill dated October 12, 1850, calling for a certain length of the main ledge "with the branches or spurs of said ledge."

[40] De la Beche, Geology of Cornwall, p. 313; Tapping, Customs of Derbyshire, (1851), p. 31.

lish term "Flitters," meaning fragments of the vein, indicated that the influence of miners from England in framing these regulations was very decided. "Flatt" diggings are mentioned in the rules of Mt. Pleasant Mining District of El Dorado County.[41] This is an unusual term used in the laws of Derbyshire.[42] The wording of the extralateral grant became very complex in the case of later regulations and we find the terms "dips, angles and spurs, offshoots, outcrops, depths, widths and variations" used to express this idea.[43]

One hundred linear feet along the ledge was during the fifties the commonest length in California for a quartz claim, but during the early sixties two hundred feet along the ledge or lead became the rule for the newer districts.[44] A few districts were formed from time to time in which square measurement of quartz claims with vertical boundaries was adhered to, but these were in the small minority. In surface width no lateral measurement whatever was specified in the earlier regulations, leaving the acquisition of sufficient surface area for convenient working of the lode to the individual locator. In fact, most of the early rules expressly prescribed a certain length of claim "without regard to width." In the late fifties and early sixties a definite width was usually prescribed but this varied from fifty feet in some districts to six hundred feet in total width in others. The latter measurement was designated in El Dorado Mining District, El Dorado County, April 7th, 1863,[44a] and is noteworthy because the Mining Act of 1872 adopted this as the maximum width for lode claims. Probably two hundred and fifty feet "on each side of the center of the lead" [45] became the commonest lateral measurement in California.

The mining regulations of the various districts of Nevada are of special interest to us because it is generally conceded that Senator Wm. M. Stewart, who represented Nevada in Congress, in framing the Act of 1866 was profoundly influenced by the miners'

---

[41] Vol. XIV, Tenth U. S. Census, p. 275.

[42] See Mander's Glossary of Derbyshire Mining Terms, etc. (1824), p. 12.

[43] Vol. XIV, Tenth U. S. Census, 310-311, 500.

[44] "Quartz claims are usually two hundred feet long following the course of the lode." Hittel, Resources of California, (1866).

[44a] Vol. XIV, Tenth Census, p. 312.

[45] This language is also of interest because the Act of 1872 provides that lode claims shall not "extend more than three hundred feet on each side of the middle of the vein at the surface." U. S. Revised Stats., § 2320.

regulations of his state. He was ably assisted by Senator Conness of California. As mining spread from California into the other parts of the West, the miners carried with them to the new "diggings" the same general ideas, organized mining districts and adopted rules and regulations similar to those existing in California. As might be expected, coming at a later period when many of the divergent views which sprang up simultaneously in different parts of the pioneer camps of California had become harmonized, the rules adopted in other Western States and territories conformed in a remarkable degree to a general type. This is particularly true of Nevada. Most of its district regulations were adopted between the years 1859 and 1866.[46] With very few exceptions these rules prescribed claims of two hundred feet in length on the lead or ledge, which, as we have seen, had become the prevailing length of lode claims in mining districts of California of the same period.[47] The extralateral grant in the Nevada regulations was also described in the same language that had originated in California.[48] The miner was entitled to his two hundred feet along the vein together with all its "dips, spurs and angles." The term "variations" was also added in some instances as well as other words such as "strings and feeders" to express the idea of the all-inclusiveness of the grant. In Nevada the extralateral feature was practically universal, a notable exception being in Eureka

---

[46] Vol XIV, Tenth U. S. Census, pp. 508-554.

[47] In Arizona claims of two hundred feet in length were quite common but the majority of the districts specified three hundred feet. Vol. XIV, Tenth U. S. Census, pp. 247-266. The districts of Utah, formed in 1863-1864, prescribed two hundred feet as the lawful length in any district noted. Id. pp. 614-625. In Colorado the customary length was one hundred feet. Colorado was further removed from the influence of the Pacific Slope and had elaborate regulations of a unique type providing for tunnel claims and possessing many features not found in the regulations of other states. Id. pp. 365-472. Neither were the words "dips, spurs, angles and variations," etc., commonly used in Colorado though they were used in all of the other States noted. The width of lode claims in these States varied as in California. Colorado already showed the tendency toward narrow claims now characteristic of that State and as early as August 21st, 1862, the rules of Bevan Mining District, Summit County, provided that lode claims shall be "twenty-five feet wide on each side of the wall rock of the crevice of said lode." Id. p. 462; see also p. 466. The Castle Dome District regulations of Yuma County, Arizona, in 1862, provided for a width of one hundred yards on each side of the vein which is the same width specified in the Act of 1872 passed by Congress ten years later.

[48] This is quite natural, for miners from California migrated, in large numbers, to Nevada and particularly to the Comstock Lode and vicinity. Lord, Comstock Mining and Miners, U. S. G. S. (1883); Browne, Mineral Resources, (1867), p. 27.

Mining District, where in 1869 the miners attempted to abolish the extralateral right and prescribed that, because of the peculiar nature of the deposits, claims should be one hundred feet square in order to avoid "expensive litigations." [49]

During most of this period, from 1850 to 1866, the state and territorial governments as already noted were satisfied to allow the miners to determine for themselves the laws which controlled their acquisition and working of mining claims. California did not legislate on the subject at all, except to approve of what the miners had done.

The legislature of Idaho, February 4, 1864, passed an act providing: [49a]

> "That any quartz claim shall consist of two hundred feet in length along the lead or lode, by one hundred feet in breadth, covering and *including all dips, spurs and angles,* etc."

This right was later expressly confined to the one lode claimed. The act was silent as to placers. [50]

A statute of Arizona effective January 1st, 1865, provided that:

> "Every mining claim or pertenencia is declared to consist of a superficial area of two hundred yards square, to be measured so as to include the principal mineral vein or mineral deposits, always having reference to and *following the dip of the vein so far as it can or may be worked,* etc."

The act was quite comprehensive and somewhat complex and shows very strong influence of the Mexican-Spanish laws, many terms of the latter being employed. It expressly excluded placer mining from its operation. [51]

A statute of Oregon of October 24, 1864, provided:

> Section I. "That any person or company of persons establishing a claim on any quartz-lead containing gold, silver, copper, tin or lead, or a claim on a vein of cinnabar, for the purpose of mining the same, shall be allowed to have, hold and possess the land or vein, with *all its dips, spurs and angles* for the distance of three hundred feet in length and seventy-five feet in width on each side of such lead or vein."

This statute also provided that only one claim on each lead

---

[49] Vol. XIV, Tenth U. S. Census, p. 551.
[49a] Browne, Mineral Resources, (1867), pp. 248-249.
[50] Act of January 12, 1865; Vol. XIV, Tenth U. S. Census, p. 135.
[51] Browne, Mineral Resources, (1867), pp. 249-257; Yale, Mining Claims, p. 84.

or vein could be held by location and expressly left the acquisition of title to placer claims to the miners' local laws.[52]

The territorial legislature of Washington on January 29th, 1863, adopted the following statute:

Section I. "That the extent of a quartz mining claim shall not exceed *two hundred feet* of the lead, including *all the dips, spurs and angles* embraced within said two hundred feet."

The territorial legislature of Montana on December 26th, 1864, enacted the following:

Section III. "Claims on any lead, lode or ledge, either of gold or silver, hereafter discovered, shall consist of not more than *two hundred feet* along the lead, lode or ledge, together with *all dips, spurs and angles* emanating or diverging from said lead, lode or ledge, as also fifty feet on each side of said lead, lode or ledge, for working purposes, etc."

The amount of ground which could be taken up on the lode was limited to one thousand feet in each direction from the discovery claim.

Colorado on November 7th, 1861, adopted a statute limiting the length of a lode claim to one hundred feet. By Act of March 11, 1864, sixteen such claims could be consolidated under one discovery and on February 9th, 1866, the length of a claim for each person was changed to fourteen hundred feet.[53]

New Mexico, on January 18th, 1865, passed an act which from the evidence at hand, appears to have limited claims to two hundred feet for each person of the length of the lode "of its entire width, *including all its dips, openings, spurs, angles and variations,* with a right to follow such vein to any depth, etc." and a total limit of one thousand five hundred feet for a company claim.[54]

A Nevada statute approved February 27th, 1866, provided that:

Section 23. ". . . No person shall be entitled to hold by location more than *two hundred feet* of any one ledge except by virtue of discovery of the same, for which he shall be entitled to hold two hundred feet additional . . . . No claim shall, in the aggregate, exceed in extent two thousand feet on any one ledge."

Section 24. "Any location made on a ledge by authority

---

[52] Vol. XIV, Tenth U. S. Census, pp. 200-201. Yale says this Oregon statute "is a mere transcript of the miners' laws regulating claims upon lodes, noticed as in force in California, and which may be found elsewhere." Yale, Mining Claims, p. 84.

[53] Morrison's Mining Rights, (14th ed.) p. 21; 1 Copp's Land Owner, 84.

[54] Vol. XIV, Tenth U. S. Census, p. 184.

of this act shall be deemed to include *all the dips, spurs, angles and variations* of said ledge.

"The locators of any ledge shall be entitled to hold one hundred feet on each side of the same, etc. . . ."

This act expressly provided that placer mining should be "subject to such regulations as the miners in the several mining districts shall adopt." [55]

It is quite evident that these state statutes were based on the local miners' laws and were merely declaratory of the existence of an extralateral right on quartz veins which right, as has been observed, had already been fully developed in the various mining districts by the miners themselves.

The Federal Mining Act of 1866.[56]

During all these years the Federal Government had remained silent on the question of the disposition of these mineral lands.[57]

---

[55] Browne, Mineral Resources, (1867), pp. 242-245.

[56] 14 U. S. Stats. at L. 251.

[57] ". . . . this system of free mining fostered by our neglect, and matured and perfected by our generous inaction." Remarks of Senator Stewart, Appendix No. 1, 70 U. S. 779. There was indirect recognition of these possessory rights of miners in a number of earlier Congressional statutes:

An Act of Congress establishing federal courts for the District of Nevada approved February 27, 1865, provided: § 9, "That no possessory action . . . . for the recovery of a mining title . . . . shall be affected by the fact that the paramount title to the land on which such mines lie is in the United States, but each case shall be adjudged by the law of possession." 13 Stats. at L., 440.

An Act of Congress of March 3, 1865, regulating the sale of town lots provided: § 2, "That where mineral veins are possessed, which possession is recognized by local authority, . . . town lots . . . shall be subject to such possession . . . . Provided, however, that nothing herein shall be construed as to recognize any color of title in possessors for mining purposes as against the government of the United States." 13 Stats. at L. 529.

An Act of Congress of May 5, 1866, concerning the boundaries of the State of Nevada provided that: "All possessory rights . . . to mining claims discovered, located and originally recorded, in compliance with the rules and regulations adopted by miners in . . . . Nevada, shall remain as valid, subsisting mining claims; but nothing herein contained shall be so construed as granting a title in fee to any mineral lands held by possessory titles in the mining states and territories." 14 Stats. at L. 43.

Treaty with Peru: Art. XIV. "Peruvian citizens shall enjoy the same privileges, in frequenting mines, and in digging or working for gold, upon the public lands situated in the State of California, as are, or may be hereafter, accorded by the United States of America to the citizens or subjects of the most favored nation." 10 U. S. Stats. at L. 926, 932. July 26, 1851.

Treaty with Tabeguache Indians: Art. III. "The right of any citizen of the United States to mine without interference or molestation in any part of the country hereby retained by said Indians [in Colorado], where gold or other metals or minerals may be found, is hereby also conferred and guaranteed." 13 U. S. Stats. at L. 673, 674. Oct. 7, 1863.

They were a part of the public domain and Congress was alone empowered by the Federal Constitution to dispose of the territory belonging to the United States.[58] Acquiescence in the extensive mining operations of these years was presumed because of this failure to act and what would otherwise have been a clear trespass on the part of the horde of invading miners was recognized by the courts as establishing a right through sufferance.[59]

There had been various attempts to induce Congress to legislate on the subject of these mineral lands and there were plans to lease them, reserving a royalty for the government,[60] and also to sell them outright at public auction to the highest bidder, thus enabling the government to pay off a portion at least of the vast debt inherited from the Civil War.[61] The miners of the West were jealous of any interference with the authority and control over the mining regions which they had been exercising for so many years.[62] But the day arrived when action by Congress could no longer be prevented, and Senator Stewart of Nevade and Senator Conness of

Treaty with Shoshonee-Goship Indians: Art. IV. "It is further agreed by the parties hereto that the country of the Goship tribe [in Montana] may be explored and prospected for gold and silver, or other minerals and metals; and when mines are discovered they may be worked, and mining and agricultural settlements formed and ranches established wherever they may be required." 13 Stats. at L. 681, 682. Oct. 12, 1863. See also Miners License Tax (1865), 13 U. S. Stats. at L. 473, and Bullion Tax (1864), 13 U. S. Stats. at L. 271-272.

[58] U. S. Const. Art. IV, § 3, subd. 2.

[59] "We cannot shut our eyes to the public history, which informs us that under this legislation (in re the State of Nevada recognizing the validity and binding force of the rules, regulations and customs of the mining districts) and not only without interference by the national government, but under its implied sanction, vast mining interests have grown up, employing many millions of capital, and contributing largely to the prosperity and improvement of the whole country." Sparrow v. Strong (1865), 70 U. S. 97, 104, 18 L. Ed. 49. "For eighteen years—from 1848 to 1866—the regulations and customs of miners, as enforced and moulded by the courts and sanctioned by the legislation of the State, constituted the law governing property in mines and in water on the public mineral lands. Until 1866, no legislation was had looking to a sale of the mineral lands." Jennison v. Kirk (1878), 98 U. S. 453, 458-459, 25 L. Ed. 240.

[60] When Senator Stewart's bill came before the Senate it contained a clause providing for payment to the government of a royalty of three per cent of the output of the mines. This was eliminated before the bill was finally passed. See Congressional Globe Debates of 1866.

[61] See Yale, Mining Claims, pp. 340-354.

[62] Whereas; since the discovery of gold in California it has been the policy of the General Government and of the different state and Territorial legislatures upon the Pacific slope (except the last legislature of this state) not to interfere with the laws and regulations of the miners in the different districts, but to permit them to enact such laws as to them seemed proper and just in regard to the government of the mines, such laws having always when tested been sanctioned and approved by the highest judicial tribunals, and,

California, realizing that they must take affirmative action if they would forestall adverse legislation by those of the Eastern States who were not in sympathy with the Western problems, prepared and introduced the bill generally known as the mining Act of 1866.[63]

This act established the free right to mine on the public domain and legalized what had theretofore been a technical trespass. Senator Conness stated in his report on the bill as chairman of the Committee on Mines and Mining:

> "By this bill it is only proposed to dispose of the vein mines. . . . . It is not proposed to interfere with, or impose any tax upon, the miners engaged in working placer mines, as those mines are readily exhausted, and not generally remunerative to those engaged in working them. . . . . (It is) an act to provide for investing the miners of the country with the fee simple to their vein mines. . . . .

Whereas; under this liberal policy the development of mineral wealth upon the Pacific Slope has been unparalleled in the history of the world, and possessing the utmost confidence in the intelligence in the mining population of this state, and their capacity for creditably continuing the time honored custom of enacting their own laws for the government of the mines free from legislative interference and,

Whereas; believing as we do that no general mining laws could be enacted that would meet the requirements of the different districts, as the varied character, size and location of the ledges in the different districts require different laws and believing that the action of the last legislature of this state, will have a tendency to bring about what we are so anxious to avoid viz:—Congressional interference by still more general legislation; and,

Whereas; many of the provisions of the state mining law are utterly impracticable in the Reese River Mining District besides placing upon us additional burthens in increased expenses and trouble in locating and recording our claims, therefore

Resolved, that the state mining law is utterly impracticable in many of its provisions, obnoxious and burthensome to the mining population generally, and especially so to the miners of Reese River District, where the peculiar formation and close proximity of the ledges render many of its provisions totally impracticable.

Resolved, that the last legislature of this state, in taking from us the right so long considered sacred, viz: that of enacting our own laws for the government of our mines, was guilty of a gross usurpation, or at least, abuse of power, unparalleled in the legislative, executive, or judicial history of the Pacific Slope.

Resolved, that we are in favor of the unconditional repeal of said law, and will vote for no person for either branch of the Legislature not pledged to vote and work for its repeal. (Adopted by mines of Nevada, March 30, 1866.)

[63] The threat of drastic legislation by opponents and the thrilling contest over the adoption of the Stewart bill, which finally passed, as well as the reason for its peculiar title, "An Act granting a right of way to ditch and canal owners, etc.," is dramatically set forth by Yale in his work on Mining Claims, pp. 9-12.

"The mass of the people living in the mines feel that the mines should be left free and open to and within the reach of the hardy explorer and adventurer without tax or impost whatever. . . . . They also fear all systems of sale lest any which should be adopted might result in monopoly. . . . . They, nevertheless, will readily acquiesce in any plan which shall confirm existing rights at reasonable rates. . . . . Another feature of the bill recommended is, that *it adopts the rules and regulations of miners in the mining districts* where the same are not in conflict with the laws of the United States. This renders secure all existing rights of property, and will prove at once a just and popular feature of the new policy. Those 'rules and regulations' are well understood, and form the basis of the present admirable system in the mining regions; arising out of necessity, they became the means adopted by the people themselves for establishing just protection to all.

"In the absence of legislation and statute law, the local courts, beginning with California, recognize those 'rules and regulations,' the central idea of which was *priority of possession,* and have given to the country rules of decision, so equitable as to be commanding in its natural justice, and to have secured universal approbation. The California reports will compare favorably, in this respect, with the history of jurisprudence in any part of the world. Thus the miners' 'rules and regulations' are not only well understood, but have beeen construed and adjudicated for now nearly a quarter of a century.

"It will be readily seen how essential it is that this great system, established by the people in their primary capacities, and evidencing by the highest possible testimony the peculiar genius of the American people for founding empire and order, shall be preserved and affirmed. Popular sovereignty is here displayed in one of its grandest aspects, and simply invites us not to destroy, but to put upon it the stamp of national power

---

Hon. E. F. Dunne of Nevada in a letter to Dr. R. W. Raymond (Dec. 20, 1869) described the situation as follows: "Fortunately, the mining interest was ably represented in Congress, led by Senators Stewart of Nevada and Conness of California, both thorough masters of the subject. They grappled the question with all their power, knowing it was a matter of life or death to the regions they represented, and, after a desperate struggle, defeated the highest bidder plan, and achieved a complete victory for the principles most anxiously desired by the miners, namely, the recognition of their mining laws, and the right of the discoverer of a mine to purchase the title from the government at a reasonable price. No matter how defective the bill may be in detail; no matter how many points it leaves entirely untouched; the miners will ever be grateful for its passage, for in that, to them, memorable session, it was not a question of detail nor perfection, but a struggle between two great conflicting principles, and the policy desired by the miners prevailed." Raymond, Mineral Resources (1870), p. 423.

and unquestioned authority."[64]

The language of Senator Wm. M. Stewart in advocating the passage of the lode law of 1866 cannot be improved upon, for it is the best evidence of his own mental operations and gives us the reasons which controlled him in framing the Act and embodying in it the extralateral grant, already a part of the miners' law. The following liberal quotation is therefore pardonable:

"To extend the pre-emption system—applicable to agricultural lands—to mines is absurd and impossible. Nature does not deposit the precious metals in rectangular forms, descending between perpendicular lines into the earth, but in veins or lodes, varying from one foot to three hundred feet in width, dipping from a perpendicular from one to eighty degrees, and coursing through mountains and ravines at nearly every point of the compass. In exploring for vein mines, it is a vein or lode that is discovered, not a quarter section of land marked by surveyed boundaries. In working a vein more or less land is required, depending upon its size, course, dip, and a great variety of other circumstances, not possible to provide for in passing general laws. Sometimes these veins are found in groups, within a few feet of each other, and dipping into the earth at an angle of from thirty to fifty degrees, as at Freiberg, Saxony, or Austin, in Nevada. In such case a person buying a single acre in a rectangular form would have several mines at the surface, and none at five hundred or a thousand feet in depth. With such a division of a mine, one owning it at the surface, another at a greater depth, neither would be justified in expending money in costly machinery, deep shafts and long tunnels, for the working of the same. Nor will it do to sell the land in advance of discovery, for this would stop explorations, and practically limit our mining wealth to the mines already found for no one would 'prospect' with much energy upon the land of another, and land speculators never find mines. The mineral lands must remain open and free to exploration and development; and while this policy is pursued our mineral resources are inexhaustible. There is room enough for every prospector who wishes to try his luck in hunting for new mines for a thousand years of exploration, and yet there will be plenty of mines undiscovered. It would be a national calamity to adopt any system that would close that region to the prospector.

"The question then presents itself, how shall the Government give title, so important for permanent prosperity, and avoid these intolerable evils? I answer, there is but one mode, and that is to assure the title to those who now or hereafter

[64] Browne, Mineral Resources, 1867, pp. 219-220.

may occupy according to local rules, suited to the character of the mines and the circumstances of each mining district. In the increasing agitation of the subject by the introduction into Congress of bills which miners regard as a system of confiscation, and which tend to destroy all confidence in mining titles, we now need statutes which shall continue the system of free mining, and hold the mineral lands open to the exploration and occupation, subject to legislation by Congress and local rules; something which recognizes the obligation of the Government to respect private rights which have grown up under its tacit consent and approval, and which shall be in harmony with the legislation of 1865, protecting possessory rights, irrespective of any paramount interest of the United States. The system will be in harmony with the rules of property as understood by a million men, with the legislation of nine States and Territories, with a course of judicial decisions extending over nearly a quarter of a century, and finally ratified and confirmed by the Supreme Court of the United States; in harmony, in short, with justice and good policy." Appendix No. 1, 70 U. S., 779, 780.

During the course of the debate in the Senate Senator Stewart said:

"He[65] evidently has not read it (the bill), and has fallen into the popular prejudice of supposing that land is to be sold in rectangular form between perpendicular lines. It has been explained that this cannot be done. A vein pitches into a hill, and a perpendicular line would cut it up into pieces. He speaks of that. This bill provides for selling the vein and following it into the earth, with its natural dips and angles."[66]

Senator Conness also added:

"I desire to say to him, (Senator Williams of Oregon) in this connection, that vein mines do not enter the earth by perpendicular lines, but on the contrary, have what are called dips or slants running by oblique lines into the earth; that they follow each other regularly in that respect; and that the custom now, and the habit everywhere, and the law, first determined by necessity, by the fact, next by the population obeying that necessity, next by the local courts affirming that necessity by their decisions, is that the miner is authorized to follow every vein according to its dips and angles and variations. This whole bill is based upon the principle of confirm-

---

[65] Referring to the writer of a letter read by an opponent of the bill in which the writer stated that it would be absurd to sell quartz mines by subdivisions with vertical boundaries because lode mines did not conform to such surface allotments. See Congressional Globe, June 18, 1866, pp. 3451-2.

[66] Congressional Globe, June 18, 1866, p. 3452.

ing what has grown out of necessity, the wisest system, perhaps, that could possibly be devised, which is the work of the people themselves. Would the senator want to enter the earth by perpendicular lines so that a man who owned a claim today, after he had descended 50 ft. of it, should leave it to the ownership of another man tomorrow?"[67]

The Act was quite universally approved in the West. The Sacramento Union of June 23, 1866, said:

" . . . . this bill has been framed with a more intelligent regard for the interests of the people of the Pacific Coast than any other previous measure that we can now recall, and it is probable that its provisions can be executed without inflicting injury upon the rights which accrued under the policy hitherto pursued by the government."

Governor McCormick of Arizona, in his annual message delivered to the legislature October 8th, 1866, said:

"The act of Congress to legalize the occupation of mineral lands, and to extend the rights of pre-emption thereto, adopted at the late session, preserves all that is best in the system created by miners themselves, and saves all vested rights under that system, while offering a permanent title to all who desire it, at a mere nominal cost. It is a more equitable and practicable measure than the people of the mineral districts had supposed Congress would adopt, and credit for its liberal and acceptable provisions is largely due to the influence of the representatives of the Pacific coast, including our own intelligent delegate. While it is not without defects, as a basis of legislation it is highly promising, and must lead to stability and method, and so inspire increased confidence and zeal in quartz mining."[68]

The Virginia Enterprise, the leading journal of the State of Nevada, on July 13, 1866, said editorially:

"The Bill proposed nothing but what already exists, except giving a perfect title to the owners of any mine who may desire it."

When we come to analyze the Act of 1866 we find that it is just what its author and others claimed for it, merely a confirmation of miners' rules and regulations with the added feature of

---

[67] Id. p. 3234. This language of Senator Conness is strikingly similar to arguments of some of the French Statesmen in the Chamber of Deputies when the French mining law of 1810 was under consideration. Halleck's translation of De Fooz on the Law of Mines had already been published (1860) on the Pacific Coast and the Senator had undoubtedly read it. See 4 California Law Review, 371-372.

[68] Browne, Mineral Resources (1867), p. 225.

affording an opportunity to the miner of securing a title in fee simple to his mining claim through issuance of a patent.

Section one of the Act confirmed what had theretofore been tacitly accepted as the fact, that mineral lands of the public domain were free to prospectors and miners, subject to statutory regulation and *"also to the local customs or rules of miners* in the several mining districts" etc.

Section two provided that when "a vein or lode of quartz, or other rock in place, bearing gold, silver, cinnabar or copper," has been taken up *"according to the local customs or rules of miners* in the district where the same is situated" and not less than one thousand dollars expended thereon,[69] the claimant might "file in the local land office a diagram of the same, so extended laterally or otherwise as *to conform to the local laws, customs, and rules of miners"* and "receive a patent therefor, granting such mine, together with the right to follow such vein or lode, *with its dips, angles and variations,*[70] *to any depth,* although it may enter the land adjoining, which land adjoining shall be sold subject to this condition."[71]

Section three is concerned with the detailed procedure for acquiring a patent.

> Section IV provided . . . . "that no location hereafter made shall exceed *two hundred feet in length along the vein* for each locator, with an additional claim for discovery to the discoverer of the lode, with the right to follow such vein *to any depth, with all its dips, variations and angles,* together

---

[69] The Reese River and other district laws of 1863 provided that "Whenever one thousand dollars shall have been expended" on a claim, it "shall be deemed as belonging in fee to the locators thereof and their assigns" etc. Senator Stewart is supposed to have modeled the Act of 1866 upon the Reese River district regulations and the fact that this precedent in the Reese River rules exists is at least corroborative evidence to support this view. Vol. XIV Tenth U. S. Census, pp. 525, 533, showing that this same principle and amount had been adopted in Placer County, California, in 1863, and in the Genoa Mining District, Nevada, during or prior to 1860. See Bancroft's Handbook of Mining (1861), p. 203. The same principle is to be noticed in Grass Valley, Nevada County, in 1852. Vol. XIV Tenth U. S. Census, p. 330. See also pp. 310-11.

[70] The Sutro Tunnel Act, 14 U. S. Stats. 242, of July 25, 1866, passed by Congress one day prior to this main lode Act of 1866 used the language "dips, spurs and angles" as applied to the Comstock lode and veins which might be intersected by the tunnel.

[71] Julien, who bitterly opposed the passage of this act in the House, said of this extralateral feature " . . . . this bill overturns the common law of the world, by allowing one man to run half a mile under the land of another." Congressional Globe (July 23, 1866), p. 4050.

with a reasonable quantity of surface for the convenient working of the same, as fixed by local rules; and provided further, that no person may make more than one location on the same lode, and not more than three thousand feet shall be taken in any one claim by any association of persons.[72]

The balance of the sections of the act related to mining matters of subordinate importance and to rights of way for ditches and canals on the public domain, etc.

It is quite clear that the act did not interfere materially with the operation of the miner's rules and customs and instead of abridging the powers of these local law-making bodies, the act repeatedly places the stamp of approval on their functions and existence[73] It is true that the act did prescribe what should be the lawful maximum length of a lode claim thereafter made but it has already been pointed out that this limitation of "two hundred feet in length along the vein for each locator"[74] had been adopted almost universally throughout the West in the mining districts and by the state and territorial legislatures, as the linear measurement for lode claims except in the older districts, where one hundred feet had been the rule. The limitation of "one location on the same lode" for each locator was also a rule in force in nearly all the districts and also adopted by the legislatures. The "additional claim for discovery to the discoverer" was also a universally accepted regulation. The granting of "the right to follow such vein or lode, with its dips, angles and variations, to any depth" was not as we have seen, the creation of a new right,[75] but

---

[72] All of these provisions were already in force in a vast majority of the mining districts, excepting possibly the last limitation of 3000 feet as the maximum length for a company. Even this was foreshadowed in local rules for a maximum length of 2400 feet had already been prescribed. Vol. XIV Tenth U. S. Census, p. 616. And see also similar legislation in Montana, (Act of Dec. 26, 1864, limiting length to 1000 feet in each direction from the discovery claim); Colorado, (Act of Mar. 11, 1864, limiting length to sixteen 100 foot claims, and Act of Feb. 9, 1866, limiting length of a claim to 1400 feet); Nevada, (Act of Feb. 27, 1866, limiting length of a claim to 2000 feet); and New Mexico, (Act of Jan. 18, 1865, limiting the length of a company claim to 1500 feet).

[73] During the course of the Senate debate on this bill, Senator Stewart said: "All there is in this bill is a simple confirmation of the existing condition of things in the mining regions, leaving everything where it was, indorsing the mining rules." Congressional Globe (June 18, 1866) p. 3234.

[74] In the bill as originally drafted, this length was 300 feet. Congressional Globe (June 18, 1866), p. 2225.

[75] The anathema that has been heaped upon the framers of the Law of Apex is amusing to one familiar with the real facts underlying its origin. "The Law of Apex, this monumental blunder of experimental legislation" . . . . "begotten in bland self-complacent ignorance by a group of opulent

was language taken bodily from the miners' rules and regulations themselves, and which had already become the "law of the land" throughout the entire West except in a few mining districts adhering to the square surface claim with vertical boundaries. The districts where the extralateral right was not in force were the rare exception, and the words "dips, spurs, angles and variations" had long since become common mining parlance[76] and were employed every day in conveyances of interests in lode claims.[77] As already noted, the legislatures of most of the Western States and Territories had, prior to the passage of the Act of 1866, also enacted statutes along the lines of the local miners' laws, and the extralateral right had become so thoroughly a part of the mining law of the West, that in 1866 to have disassociated the idea of extralateral right from lode mining would have been unthinkable.[78] If Senator Stewart, on whose head so much uninformed abuse has been undeservedly heaped, had in 1866 urged Congress to abolish the extralateral right, instead of urging its acceptance, not only his Nevada constituents, but the first mining community he happened to pass through on his return from Washington would undoubtedly

---

mechanics" . . . . guilty of "foisting upon the mining public of a great domain your ill-advised and flimsy statutes,"—so writes a critic in Economic Geology, Vol. I, No. 6 (July, 1906), p. 572 et seq. Usually this crime is charged on Senator Stewart who framed the Act and took a leading part in the Comstock litigation. As late as the issue of June 10, 1916, the Mining & Scientific Press (p. 850) contains a letter from a correspondent in which he refers to "the principle of the extralateral right as having been evolved from the brain of a capable, brilliant lawyer and through his remarkable ability and powers of persuasion made to serve his ends," and adds "it has continued on its pernicious course nearly 50 years." The shades of the pioneers of 1851 would resent such credit being given to a lawyer fifteen years later, for in many of the mining camps, lawyers were expressly prohibited from practicing. "No lawyer shall be permitted to practice law in any court in the district under penalty of not more than fifty nor less than twenty lashes and be forever banished from the district." (By-laws of Dec. 10, 1860, Union Mining District, Clear Creek County, Colorado. Vol. XIV Tenth U. S. Census, p. 373. See also, p. 411). This is one original sin which the lawyers cannot be charged with. They usually frame most legislation but the democratic mining camp usurped this privilege in the case of the extralateral right.

[76] See Bullion Mining Co. v. Croesus Mining Co. (1866), 2 Nev. 168, 176. Mark Twain wrote: "I have been through the California mill, with all its dips, spurs and angles, variations and sinuosities. I have worked there at all the different trades known to the catalogue." American Stationer.

[77] Congdon's Mining Laws and Forms (1864), p. 168, San Francisco, uses the words "dips, spurs and angles" in standard form of mining deed.

[78] As Senator Conness said in the Senate debate on the part of the bill conferring extralateral rights: "That simply is no change; it is the law of the mines now." Congressional Globe (June 18, 1866) p. 3234.

have met him with a delegation, politely described in the pioneer days as a "neck-tie party," or at least they would have carried a rail and a goodly supply of tar and feathers. To have ignored the extralateral right in those days would have meant to unsettle the title to virtually all of the countless thousands of lode claims which had already been acquired throughout the West. If any sin was committed in perpetuating the extralateral right, the pioneer miners of the West, and the legislatures of the Western States and Territories, and not Senator Stewart, were primarily responsible. All that he added to the laws created by these pioneers, was the privilege of securing a fee simple title through patent. Whether they accepted even this desirable feature or not remained entirely optional with them, for they might continue to hold their claims under the possessory title afforded by their locations exactly as they had been doing up to that time under their own local laws. A very few districts had to change their rules and recognize that quartz locations made after the passage of the act[79] must conform to the prescribed two hundred foot length along the lode for each claimant, but as we have seen, this had already become the universally accepted length and most of the state and territorial laws had already anticipated the federal act, so this limitation was not an innovation. The extralateral right as already noted, had also become a characteristic feature of practically all of the mining districts and the Act of 1866 in recognizing it, continued the grant of the right in the identical language employed by the great majority of the local regulations and western legislatures so that few districts had to change their laws in this respect.[80]

It is not the province of this article to discuss the workings of the Act of 1866 and the interpretation placed by the courts on the rights conferred by the Act. The very excellent treatises on the subject of mining law are referred to for this information.[81] It is interesting to note in passing, that the Act of 1866 did not prescribe the manner of determining the direction of the end bound-

---

[79] Claims located prior to the passage of the Act were governed by the local laws as to length. 1 Copp's Land Owner, p. 83.

[80] "Usually a quartz claim follows the lode as deep into the earth as it may go", (p. 184) . . . . "quartz claims ordinarily follow the lode, with its dips and angles, to the full extent of its depth," (p. 186). Hittell, Hand Book of Mining for the Pacific States (1861).

[81] Lindley on Mines (3rd ed. 1914), §§ 53-61, 566-577a; Costigan on Mining Law (1908), pp. 14-18, 415-417; Morrison's Mining Rights (14th ed. 1910), p. 198.

aries of the length of vein located. Naturally the ascertainment of the longitudinal limits of the segment of vein carved out in depth, became important. The land department issued instructions providing that when not agreed upon between adjoining claimants nor fixed by local rules, the end lines "shall be drawn at right angles to the ascertained or apparent general course of the vein or lode."[82] It is strange that none of the district regulations seem to have provided the method of determining the exact measure of this right to mine in depth. Judge Field in the celebrated Eureka Case[83] stated the proposition as if it were one already generally accepted, that,

> "Lines drawn down through the ledge or lode at right angles with a line representing this general course at the end of the claimant's line of location will carve out, so to speak, a section of the ledge or lode within which he is permitted to work and out of which he cannot pass."

This view was later upheld in the Argonaut-Kennedy case.[84] The interesting feature of this situation is the fact that in both Derbyshire and in Germany the laws granting the extralateral right were equally indefinite regarding these end bounding planes and in each country the generally accepted custom was to lay out the end line planes at right angles to the general course of the vein.[85]

The Act of 1866 was also found wanting in other respects. The fact that no lateral surface width for a claim was prescribed by its terms gave rise to great confusion and resulted in applications for patents for claims of all conceivable shapes.[86] The restriction that only one lode or vein could be owned in a claim also gave rise to endless disputes and litigation.[87]

No one had claimed that the Act of 1866 was perfect. It was hastily prepared to forestall contemplated drastic legislation which would have seriously crippled the mining industry in the West and

[82] Yale, Mining Claims, p. 360.

[83] (1877), 4 Sawy. 302, Fed. Cas. 4548.

[84] Argonaut Mining Co. v. Kennedy Mining Co. (1900), 131 Cal. 15, 63 Pac. 148, affirmed on other grounds in Kennedy Mining Co. v. Argonaut Mining Co. (1903), 189 U. S. 1, 47 L. Ed. 685. This decision was the first to definitely determine the extent of the extralateral grant, and was rendered fifty years after the right was initiated. See also pp. 99, 52, Lord U. S. G. S. Monograph IV.

[85] 4 California Law Review, 366, 375-6, n. 13 and 14, 378, n. 42.

[86] See Lindley on Mines, § 59.

[87] Senator Stewart remarked in the debate on the Act of 1872: "Now, for want of a more definite rule the whole region is in litigation. Every man who goes West to locate a claim finds so much local legislation which is uncertain that he is discouraged; he finds the neighborhood in litigation."

was generally recognized as being crude and incomplete, though "a step in the right direction." Senator Stewart later prepared a bill calculated to remedy the objections to the Act of 1866 already noted, and which passed the Senate, February 8th, 1871, but failed in the House for lack of time.[88] This bill contained many of the features of the subsequent Act which was adopted in 1872. It contained an interesting clause not found in the Act of 1872, providing not only that the end lines should be parallel but also that they should be "at right angles with the general course of the vein."[89]

A discussion of the Federal Act of 1872 which superseded the Act of 1866 and which is the mining law now in force in the Western States is appropriately reserved for separate presentation.

Wm. E. Colby.

Berkeley, California.

The various objections to the Act of 1866 and a detailed discussion of its shortcomings as well as recommendations for curative legislation are to be found in Raymond, Mineral Resources (1870), pp. 421-444.

[88] Senator Stewart in the debate that preceded its passage in the Senate said: "This bill makes no change in the principles of legislation heretofore had as to mining claims, except that it limits in certain instances the rights of miners to make laws for themselves and defines the shape of their claims more definitely. It is a bill that has been sent out five or six times in various forms through the mining states and territories." Congressional Globe, February 8, 1871.

[89] This bill is set forth in Raymond, Mineral Resources (1872), pp. 496-499, and is followed by an interesting comment by Raymond, pp. 499-502. Dr. Raymond had already prepared a draft of a bill along similar lines. Mineral Resources, (1870), pp. 442-444. Hon. E. F. Dunne of Nevada, at Raymond's request, had also prepared a bill providing that the owner of a patented claim might follow his vein into the tract adjoining and "shall be entitled to all mineral within twenty feet of the walls of said vein." (Id. p. 436). This is the only suggestion of the adoption in America of the Germanic form of extralateral right that has come to the writer's attention.

California Law Review

Volume V   NOVEMBER, 1916   Number 1

The Extralateral Right: Shall It Be Abolished?

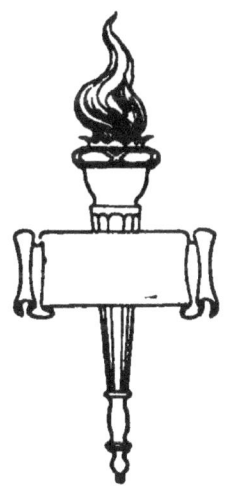

The Extralateral Right: Shall It Be Abolished?

III. The Federal Mining Act of 1872.

It was generally recognized that the law of 1866 was a long step in the right direction, inasmuch as it gave explicit federal sanction to mining on the public domain and thus set at rest any question as to what attitude the government would take toward the miners who were for eighteen years prior to its passage technical trespassers.[1] Everyone recognized that the Act of 1866 had been hastily prepared and passed to meet an emergency and thus forestall legislation hostile to the mining interests. Senator Stewart himself in urging the bill of 1871 in the Senate referred to the bill "as an amendment to the law of 1866 that was passed through in rather a crude state."[2] In the next Congress Senator Stewart was again the leader in framing the bill which during that session became the Act of 1872 and was its most active champion. A draft of a proposed act had previously been sent through the mining districts for criticism and the discussion had covered a period of two or three years.

The bill which had passed the Senate in 1871 was reintroduced in the next session of Congress and passed the House.[3] This bill

---

[1] A similar situation has but recently arisen on the public domain in connection with the immensely valuable oil lands of California and Wyoming. Oil miners had gone on the public lands, though in this case at the invitation of the government, and expended fortunes in some instances in developing oil. The placer mining law was plainly unsuited to these novel conditions, where discovery of the oil lying at great depth required large capital and considerable time. Many claimants failed to comply with all of the technical requirements of this law and while certain remedial legislation was passed by Congress to improve the situation, the federal government has more recently treated these operators as trespassers and now seeks not only to eject them from these lands but also to recover the value of the oil theretofore extracted. This reversal of the liberal policy adopted by Congress in 1866 is due to the growth of the idea that the best interests of the public demands the reservation and control by the federal government of all natural resources which are vital to the future welfare of the nation and that this new policy is especially applicable to lands containing petroleum which is in demand for use in the navy. 3 California Law Review, 272-291.

[2] Congressional Globe, Feb. 6, 1871, p. 978.

[3] Dr. Raymond in commenting on this bill said: "In its main features it is an eminently wise and salutary measure. Senator Stewart has displayed both courage and judgment in its preparation, and has given new proof of intelligent, earnest devotion to the true interests of the mining industry. Raymond, Mineral Resources (1872), p. 502.

left the length of lode claims the same as under the Act of 1866 but provided for a maximum width of three hundred feet on each side of the middle of the vein at the surface and prescribed that the end lines should be parallel and at right angles with the general course of the vein.[4]

After the bill had passed the House, the Senate Committee on Mines and Mining evidently did its real work. The various features of the law that required changing were extensively debated. There appeared before this Committee representatives of the mining interests of the West.

Senator Alcorn of Mississippi had charge of the bill as chairman of the Committee and while disclaiming any special knowledge of the subject, yet, as a matter of accomodation, stood sponsor for the measure when it came before the Senate, saying:

> "This bill has been considered by the Committee with great care, each section of the bill has been discussed, and the result is that the report embodies the intelligence brought to the Committee by various persons who appeared before it in the interests of the mining districts. . . . . As to its practical working, I will only say that it is in conformity with what seems to be the settled policy of the Government with regard to mining."[5]

Senator Stewart, who was the real advocate of the bill in its revised form—the form which was substituted for the House bill, already passed by that body,—outlined the general situation leading up to its framing as finally presented for passage. His years of experience with actual conditions

---

[4] Congressional Globe (Jan. 23, 1872), p. 533. Mr. Sargent representing California, who had charge of this bill in the House, urged its passage saying: " . . . . The bill does not make any important changes in the mining laws as they have heretofore existed. It does not change in the slightest degree the policy of the Government in the disposition of the mining lands. . . . . Now, although the legislation of 1866 was extremely imperfect in the machinery, which since that time we have been trying to improve so that it might be easier for miners to avail themselves of the benefits intended to be conferred upon them by law, yet it showed to observers that the system was correct. . . . . This bill simply oils the machinery a little; it does not change the principles of the law; it does not change the tenures; . . . . Congressional Globe, Feb. 6, 1871, p. 978.

In urging the passage of the Placer Act of 1870, Sargent had used the following language in describing the origin of these mining laws: "The original title or possession depended upon mining laws—a code originally written, modified afterward by custom—a code as well settled and understood by our courts and by the miners themselves as is the Common Law of England by the Courts of the United States—a code eminent for its wisdom, perfected by long experience, and admirably adapted to the conditions and necessities of the people among whom it originated."

[5] Congressional Globe, April 16, 1872, p. 2460.

in the mining districts of the West and his active interest in mining legislation, ever since he took the leading part in securing the adoption of the Act of 1866, add immeasurably to the weight of his views, which were as follows:

> " . . . . In the first instance the miners legislated for themselves. Congress finally in 1866 passed a bill embodying many of the principles of this bill, and from that time to this the Land Office has been operating under it, and for the last three years we have been attempting to codify it and bring it into a shape that will be satisfactory and more certain and correct abuses. Last year a bill was introduced here and passed which was quite similar to this. A bill has passed the House which is similar to the one that passed here last winter. Since its passage by the House the Delegates from the Territories and those familiar with mining rules have had a great many meetings over this bill in connection with the Committee on Mines and Mining, and the result is a codification, which is the best they can do. I believe it will meet with universal favor. It is a very important bill to be passed to prevent litigation and give certainty to mining enterprises. It provides for a very large district of country where there are important interests dependent upon it which are now in a very uncertain condition involving litigation. This is the best we can get with all the experience we can bring to bear. It is no one man's work, but it is the work of a great many men interested in this business. . . . ."[6]

When the bill as amended in the Senate came up in the House for re-passage, Representative Sargent of California made the following comment:

> ". . . . the variations from the bill as passed by the House are very trifling. . . . .[7] In the Senate the Committee on Mines and Mining and the Delegates and members of the House from the mining Territories and States, aided that Committee in perfecting the bill and improving its machinery. The bill is now entirely satisfactory to every Delegate and every member of the mining States and Territories, as well as to the Committee on Mines and Mining of this House."[8]

The bill as amended passed without any great opposition. In fact the main debate and criticism came from Western members of Congress who were not entirely satisfied with some of the changes made in the original bill by the Senate amendments. The

---

[6] Id. p. 2457.
[7] As a matter of fact they were not as trifling as Mr. Sargent would have led his colleagues to believe.
[8] Id. p. 2897.

right of free mining was not seriously challenged and the subject of the extralateral right which was again confirmed by the new act was not mentioned in the debates in Congress, an indication that no objections of consequence had as yet been made against the continued exercise of this right.[9]

The Act of 1872,[10] again confirmed the right of free mining on the public domain that had already been recognized in the Act of 1866. While the Act of 1872 was intended to limit the operation of the miners' rules and regulations and make the mining law throughout the West more uniform by prescribing in greater detail the specific acts of location, yet the first section of the act expressly provided that mineral lands might be acquired

"under regulations prescribed by law, and according to the local customs or rules of miners, in the several mining districts, so far as the same are applicable and not inconsistent with the laws of the United States."

In this connection the following was said during the Senate debate on the bill:

Mr. Trumbull (of Illinois).

" . . . . as I understand, it adopts as law the regulations which the miners may make, which may be as various as the mines."

Mr. Stewart.

"Allow me to say that the old law (Act of 1866) adopts them. One of the difficulties is that they have legislated too extensively since the adoption of that law. This curtails their power of legislation, cuts it down to to a very small extent, takes away most of it, takes anything that can be prejudicial, and prescribes the rule so that their legislation cannot interfere with it. That is the main object of the bill."

Section 2, provided that quartz or lode claims theretofore located should be

"governed as to length along the vein or lode by the customs, regulations, and laws in force at the date of their location.

---

[9] When the Placer Act of 1870 was before the House, Julien of Ohio, who had bitterly opposed the passage of the Act of 1866, could not resist the opportunity to vent again his hostility, and speaking of the extralateral grant of the latter Act said: "I admit that there may be a hardship in allowing a man to discover and hold a lode or vein of mineral which can be traced to the land of another from which he is debarred. There is hardship in that; but there is far greater hardship in the law as it now stands, recognizing the right everywhere to pursue a vein or lode on the land of another, inasmuch as it breeds interminable litigation and never can be resorted to as a method of settling titles to these lands." Congressional Globe, March 17, 1870, p. 2029.

[10] U. S. Stats. at Large, p. 91 et seq.

A mining claim located after the passage of this Act, whether located by one or more persons, may equal, but shall not exceed, one thousand five hundred feet in length along the vein or lode. . . . ."

As already noted, when the bill to amend the Act of 1866 passed the Senate in the previous session of Congress, and when the bill, which, as afterwards amended, became the Act of 1872, was reintroduced in the next session and first passed the House, it left the length of the lode claims unchanged, that is, two hundred feet along the vein for each locator and a maximum length of three thousand feet in one claim for an association of persons. The reasons for making this change were stated by Senator Stewart in the course of the debate on the bill to be as follows:

" . . . . In the Act of 1866 it is true that the locator was confined to two hundred feet, and two hundred feet additional for the discoverer of the lode, making four hundred feet. It allowed him to unite in companies until they got three thousand feet. In practical operation it is thought by the Delegates generally, and that is the experience, that three thousand feet is longer than can be worked at one place conveniently, but fifteen hundred feet makes a very reasonable claim. The practice under the other law was for them to put in fictitious names and buy them out, and you could not prevent them doing it. This matter was discussed considerably; we had several meetings on this point and the committee thought it was best to let them do directly what was reasonable, and not have them do anything indirectly.[11] It is a matter to which I am not especially wedded, but it was the result of three or four meetings of all the parties interested as to which plan should be adopted, and this was the one which was selected."

Mr. Cole, (one of the Senators from California).

"I have heard the Senator's explanation, and it is not satisfactory to me at all, because I know by the rules of miners claiming the mines upon these ledges for a long time,

---

[11] It is worth noting that this same act amended the Placer Act of 1870 by reducing the amount of ground that an individual could locate from 160 acres to 20 acres and by providing that an association of eight persons was necessary to locate 160 acres in one claim. Revised Stats., § 2330. This change gave rise to the same use of fictitious names or "dummies" in the case of placers, that Senator Stewart points out had occurred in the case of lodes, in order that an individual might acquire indirectly what the law prohibited him from acquiring directly. It is strange that this defect in the lode law should have been remedied by the same statute that injected it into the placer law. It was due to the fact that Mr. Cole of California, who evidently did not believe in large claims and who had objected to the increase of length of lode claims from 200 feet to 1500 feet, insisted on reducing the placer area an individual might locate from 160 to 20 acres. See Congressional Globe.

two hundred feet was the limit to which they restricted each other, and to allow persons now to obtain title, each individual to fifteen hundred feet upon the lode, is certainly a very great leap forward. It is in my judgment too much of an extension."[12]

Mr. Casserly:—"Does the Senator (Stewart) consider that there is no danger of abuse in allowing so great a quantity?"

Mr. Stewart—"None in the world."[13]

Another clause of Section 2 provided that "no claim shall extend more than three hundred feet on each side of the middle of the vein at the surface," and no mining regulation was permitted to reduce the width to less than twenty-five feet on each side of the vein. This provision was an attempt to bring uniformity out of the chaotic condition previously existing under the Act of 1866, which had only prescribed a uniform linear measurement along the vein and had left the determination of the surface area accompanying the vein to be determined by local laws. The Act of 1866 had granted a certain length of lode, but the shape and size of the surface area of the claim were incidental, while the Act of 1872 granted a surface area of prescribed dimensions containing the lode.[14] The intention of the miners under their earlier regulations prior to 1866, judging from the phraseology of the rules and their lack of regard for lateral surface measurements, was undoubtedly to secure to the locator a certain length of lode irrespective of the surface containing it.[15] The courts later held, however, that a patent granted under the Act of 1866 conveyed rights only to the length of lode actually included in the surface boundaries of the claim as patented, and the fact that greater number of linear feet along the lode was claimed under the rules and regulations of miners did not give the claimant any right to any portion of the length of the lode outside of his surface lines.[16] The Act of 1872 cleared up this objectionable situation by emphasizing the surface and prescribing a definite and conventional surface area which was theoretically, at least, to include the middle of the vein at the sur-

[12] Congressional Globe, April 16, 1872, p. 2458.
[13] Id. p. 2462.
[14] Lindley on Mines, § 71; Gleeson v. Martin White M. Co. (1878), 13 Nev. 442.
[15] " . . . . the claim was of so much of the lode in whatever direction it might be found to run, with a strip of the adjacent surface, taken for convenience in working the lode and as a mere incident or appurtenance thereto." Beatty, Report of Public Land Commission (1880), p. 397.
[16] This situation and its development is comprehensively treated in Lindley on Mines, §§ 58-60.

face. As was stated by Dr. Raymond in his comment on the Act of 1872:

> "The section giving absolute title to a certain surface and and all veins 'topping' within vertical lines drawn from the boundaries of that surface-claim, is necessary to prevent special litigation."[17]

This surface provision of the Act of 1872 was but the adoption of a stereotyped form of surface measurement for lode claims that had been in existence for centuries in the Germanic and Derbyshire lode mining laws. Under these latter laws a specified surface width on each side of the vein at the surface was the prescribed mode of laying out lode claims.[18] Whether these foreign laws served as a model in this respect is doubtful. There is nothing in the Congressional debates on the bill which gives us information on this point and the hearings of the Committee on Mines and Mining where the source of the provision might have been noted are not available. It has already been mentioned that many of the mining district regulations prescribed the maximum width of lode claims which should be measured "on each side of the center of the lead," and that in some of them as well as in the territorial legislation of Arizona a maximum total width of six hundred feet or two hundred yards for each claim had been prescribed.[19] It is probable that this provision of the Act of 1872 was patterned after these local laws.

A very interesting feature of Section 2 of the Act of 1872 was the concluding provision of that section providing that "The end lines of each claim shall be parallel to each other." The Act of 1866 was silent on the subject of end lines of lode locations and as a consequnce end lines of locations made under the Act were seldom parallel and often broken and of varying length. As Justice Field stated in the Eureka case,[20] end lines or rather end line planes at right angles to the general course of the vein were implied under the Act of 1866.[21] A careful search of local rules and state

---

[17] Raymond, Mineral Resources (1873), p. 453.
[18] 4 California Law Review, pp. 365-6, 375.
[19] Id. pp. 448-450.
[20] (1877), 4 Sawy. 302; Fed. Cas. 4548.
[21] The Germanic and Derbyshire laws were equally silent on this subject of the manner of making end line measurements and yet each of these laws was interpreted to impliedly confer extralateral rights between end line planes at right angles to the general course of the vein. Even under the Spanish mining ordinances of 1783, the surface claim was a rectangle with end lines, theoretically, at least, at right angles to the course of the vein. See 4 California Law Review, pp. 366-7, 375-6, 383.

and territorial legislation fails to disclose any which provided that the end lines of locations should be either at right angles to the general course of the vein or that they should be parallel, except the territorial laws of Arizona which called for lode locations with a surface two hundred yards square and the right to follow the vein on its dip. Attention has been called to the fact that the bill introduced in Congress in 1871 and the similar bill as originally introduced in the next session, which eventually, as amended, became the Act of 1872, provided that the end lines should be parallel "and at right angles with the general course of the vein," thus adopting what had theretofore been commonly accepted as the legal longitudinal limitation of the segment of vein located. Why the right angle end line provision was eliminated from the bill as finally adopted and only the requirement of parallelism retained does not appear in the debates and was probably determined upon at the unreported hearings in Committee. Evidently the idea was to permit the locator to lay out his parallel end lines in any direction and thus enable him to follow down on a valuable ore shoot in the vein which might trend or rake away from the true dip or perpendicular. If this was the intention, it was "putting the cart before the horse," for it is rarely that the locator at the time of location has any idea where ore shoots exist in the piece of vein he locates and much more rarely that he knows their trend. End lines might after location be readjusted as to direction and in this manner the locator might be enabled to include within his extralateral sweep a valuable ore shoot subsequently discovered and to follow it down. In practice, however, by the time the facts are discovered, contiguous locations on the apex of the vein will usually prevent such readjustment. It would seem to have been preferable to have retained the right angle end line requirement, for under such a rule end lines of locations placed along the apex of a vein would be more nearly uniform in direction, and conflicting extralateral rights in depth much less frequent. Of course, a decided change in the direction or course of the vein at the surface would have produced underground conflicts if the requirement of end lines at right angles to the local course of the vein were strictly followed. But the language of the earlier mining bill called for right angle measurement to be made from "the *general* course of the vein." If this wording had been retained in the Act as finally passed it would certainly have materially lessened the litigation directly traceable to the extralateral right provision. By laying out a base line on the surface representing the general course of the vein, as was done on the Comstock lode and also for a time in Australia, then projecting the end lines of the various claims taken up along the vein at right angles to this base line, and thus measuring the extent of each locator's right to follow the vein extralaterally down on its dip, there would have been afforded the most scientific and harmonious measure of this right possible to devise.[22]

Section 3 of the Act of 1872 is as follows:[23]

"That the locators of all mining locations heretofore made, or which shall hereafter be made, on any mineral vein, lode, or ledge, situated on the public domain, their heirs and assigns, where no adverse claim exists at the passage of this act, so long as they comply with the laws of the United States and the state, territorial, and local regulations, not in conflict with said laws of the United States, governing their possessory title, shall have the exclusive right of possession and enjoyment of all the surface included within the lines of their locations and of all veins, lodes, and ledges, throughout their entire depth, the top or apex of which lies inside of such surface lines extended downward vertically, although such veins, lodes, or ledges may so far depart from a perpendicular in their course downward as to extend outside the vertical side-lines of said surface locations; provided, that their right of possession to such outside parts of said veins or ledges shall be confined to such portions thereof as lie between vertical planes drawn downward as aforesaid, through the end-lines of their locations, so continued in their own direction that such planes will intersect such exterior parts of said veins or ledges. And provided further, that nothing in this section shall authorize the locator or possessor of a vein or lode which extends, in its downward course, beyond the vertical lines of his claim, to enter upon the surface of a claim owned or possessed by another."

This section is identical with Section 3 of the bill which passed the Senate in 1871. It merely confirms in more elaborate and explicit language the right which had been created by the early miners, subsequently written into their local regulations and state and territorial legislation, and later recognized in the Act of 1866. The only point of material difference was the extension of this right under the Act of 1872 to "all veins" which were found to

---

[22] See "The Law of Apex" (1914) by Kenney, a volume devoted to an expostion of this interesting principle. Also see 4 California Law Review, p. 385.
[23] See U. S. Revised Stats., § 2322.

apex within the surface of each location. The Act of 1866 had confined the extralateral right to the one main vein. This had given rise to so much uncertainty and litigation that it was deemed best to extend the right to all veins occurring in the surface area located, thus removing the temptation to trespass on another's claim in the attempt to discover or locate a secondary vein which might exist therein.[24]

The use of the words "top" or "apex" with reference to the veins found in the surface location, appears to have been the first use of these terms in this relation.[25] The miners' regulations the state and territorial legislation and the Act of 1866, all provided for the location of a specific "length along the vein." It was taken for granted that this meant that the location should include the outcrop or "top or apex" of the vein or that portion of its upper or terminal edge lying nearest the surface.[26] With the appearance of these terms in the Act of 1872 came into existence the expression the "Law of the Apex," which has since been extensively used to describe the extralateral right feature of the Act. The use of these terms, however, did not change the character of the extralateral right one iota; they were merely descriptive of a portion of the vein which it had always been assumed must form the basis of the location.

This discussion is concerned only with those portions of the Act which have a direct bearing on the extralateral right. Section 4 granted a unique tunnel right which included the right to such veins or lodes as might be discovered in the tunnel.[27] Aside from a provision contained in Section 11 applicable to veins found to exist in placer claims and Section 14 which provided that priority of title should govern where veins intersected or crossed each other and also where they united in depth, the Act was devoted to other subjects than the extralateral right.

---

[24] "The law of 1866 was fatally deficient . . . . in failing to prohibit prospecting within the surface-lines of an already located claim" but the amendment of 1872 may be considered ample to remedy this defect. Raymond, Mineral Resources (1874), p. 513. See also Raymond, Mineral Resources (1870), pp. 433-436.

[25] Stevens v. Williams (1879), Fed. Cas. No. 13,414. For a complete discussion of these terms, see Lindley on Mines, §§ 305-313.

[26] The Derbyshire and Germanic laws only called for a certain length of vein and there was no attempt to define the portion of the vein to be located. It was assumed that this would be the top or upper edge of the vein.

[27] This provision was included for the protection of certain Colorado miners. Senator Stewart in Congressional Globe (1872), pp. 978-9.

Looking at the Act of 1872 broadly we see that the fundamental principles created by the miners under their own laws and customs, later embodied in state and territorial legislation and eventually crystallized in the Act of 1866, were not materially altered by the Act of 1872.[28] The basic right of free mining was retained unchanged and the extralateral right was again confirmed, though in more elaborate language. With the exception of the parallel end line provision which supplanted the implied right angle end line measurement under the previous law and the grant of *all* veins found apexing in the surface location, the extralateral right remained the same in substance. As already noted, the surface area obtainable under the new act was described with great detail. The adoption of the basic features of the miners' laws, and the elaborate provision contained in the Act governing acquisition of the surface claim rendered the local rules and regulations of the mining districts practically obsolete. Though the Act recognized such local laws and customs as did not conflict with the federal Act their value was largely a thing of the past. They had served their important purpose and they gradually died a natural death.

The Act of 1872 was generally considered a great improvement over the imperfect and incomplete Act of 1866.[29]

It was later codified and became a part of the federal Revised Statutes,[30] and is, with a few minor additions and modifications, the mining law in force today governing the acquisition of mineral lands on the public domain. The extralateral right feature of the Act has remained unchanged. It is not the purpose of this article to present the detailed interpretation of this extra-

---

[28] "It (the Act of 1872) recognized the essential principles found in the miners' regulations." Charles J. Hughes, Jr., Address on "The Evolution of Mining Law." XXIV, Reports of American Bar Association (1901), p. 344.

[29] Judge Beatty said in the Gleeson v. Martin White M. Co. case, supra, n. 14, referring to the Act of 1872: "Nobody can pretend that it is perfect; but to our minds it is a great improvement on the system which it displaced."

Dr. Raymond in commenting on the Act, wrote: "It embodies much that I have advocated in former reports, and I think it will be approved by the large body of practical miners in the United States, who whatever criticisms they may make upon particular provisions, must agree in commending the tone which mining legislation has assumed, and the character of the protection offered to their property." After making some minor criticisms of features of the law, he added: "Nevertheless it is certain that the present law is a great advance on anything we have had." Raymond, Mineral Resources (1873), p. 454.

[30] §§ 2319-2337.

lateral grant, gradually built up by court decisions. This may be found in the leading works dealing with the subject of mining law.[31]

Before taking up the concluding phase of this discussion, which will be a consideration of the proposed abolition of the extralateral right, it may be worth while to sum up briefly the evidence bearing on the origin of the extralateral right in the United States.

If the miners' rules and regulations were patterned after mining laws of other countries we have no direct evidence bearing on the question. There were men, however, who would have been likely to have possessed some information on this subject if it had existed. Senator Wm. M. Stewart who, as we have seen, not only took the leading part in framing the Act of 1866, but also did more than anyone else in drafting the Act of 1872, had spent years in the mining districts and associated with other Senators and Congressmen from the West who aided in moulding this legislation and, as the debates reported in the Congressional Globe of that period show, were, many of them, originally miners themselves. Senator Stewart also met with delegations of miners from the Western States and Territories and discussed extensively all of the features of the mining law.

Stephen J. Field had grown up with the mining districts. He represented the miners in the California State legislature in 1851, and secured the enactment of the section of the Practice Act making the customs, usages and regulations of the "bar or diggings" govern in actions respecting mining claims. He had previously been an alcalde and later went from the supreme bench of the State to the Supreme Court of the United States. As Judge Lindley has said in his eloquent tribute to Justice Field, he had "the practical knowledge acquired by personal contact with the mining communities" and "was a part of the history of which he wrote."[32]

Justice Wm. H. Beatty was for years a district judge in the mining regions of Nevada and became the Chief Justice of the Supreme Court of that state and later, up to the date of his recent death, was Chief Justice of the Supreme Court of Cali-

---

[31] Lindley on Mines, §§ 581-615; Costigan, Mining Law, pp. 417-452; Barringer & Adams Law of Mines, pp. 437-470; Morrison, Mining Rights, (14th ed.), pp. 192-219; 1 California Law Review, pp. 336-358.
[32] Lindley on Mines, § 44.

fornia. He was greatly interested in the miners' rules and regulations and thoroughly conversant with their history.

These three men were pre-eminently qualified to discuss the evolution of the mining law of the West; each of them was deeply interested in its origin and development and they were constantly in direct contact with the pioneer miners and discussed problems arising out of the mining industry. One or the other of these men would surely have learned of the source of these local laws if this source were directly traceable to mining laws of other countries. On the contrary, we nowhere find in their remarkably lucid and complete presentations of the history and development of these laws any reference whatsoever to any foreign mining law as furnishing the basis for these early customs and regulations.

Senator Stewart in his famous speech in the United States Senate advocating the passage of the Act of 1866, described the exciting emigration to California following upon the discovery of gold, saying:

"Upon the discovery of gold in California, in 1848, a large emigration of young men immediately rushed to the modern Ophir. These people, numbering in a few months hundreds of thousands, on arriving at their future home found no laws governing the possession and occupation of mines but the common law of right, which Americans alone are educated to administer. They were forced by the very necessity of the case to make laws for themselves. The reason and justice of the laws they formed challenge the admiration of all who investigate them. Each mining district, in an area extending over not less than fifty thousand square miles, formed its own rules and adopted its own customs. The similarity of these rules and customs throughout the entire mining region was so great as to attain all the beneficial results of well-digested, general laws. These regulations were thoroughly democratic in their character, guarding against every form of monopoly, and requiring continued work and occupation in good faith to constitute a valid possession."[33]

Nowhere in his entire eloquent appeal for recognition of the principles established by the miners themselves, with its many detailed references to the democratic origin of these rules, does Senator Stewart mention their having been patterned after mining laws of other countries.

---

[33] 70 U. S. 777, Appendix.

In his classic description of the gold rush to California, Justice Field, speaking of the pioneers, says:

"Wherever they went, they carried with them that love of order and system and of fair dealing which are the prominent characteristics of our people. In every district which they occupied they framed certain rules for their government, by which the extent of ground they could severally hold for mining was designated," etc. . . . . They were so framed as to secure to all comers,, within practicable limits absolute equality of right and privilege in working mines. Nothing but such equality would have been tolerated by the miners, who were emphatically the lawmakers, as respects mining, upon the public lands in the State."[84]

Justice Field above all others should have known whether these laws were of foreign origin and yet he makes no reference to any such source.

Justice Beatty while Chief Justice of the Supreme Court of Nevada was requested by the Public Land Commission to give his views on the mining laws.[85] From his comprehensive and illuminating reply the following is quoted:[86]

"When placer mining began in California there was no law regulating the size of claims or the manner of holding and working them, and local regulations by the miners themselves became a necessity. They were adopted, not because the subject was too complicated or difficult for general regulation, but because they were needed at once as the sole refuge from anarchy. The first and most important matter to be regulated was the size of claims, and the earliest miners' rules contained little else than a limitation of the maximum amount of mining ground that one miner might hold."

He outlined the addition of other requirements to the placer rules and then added:

"After these regulations had been some time in force came the discovery of veins or lodes of gold-bearing rock in place, and to them the law of the placer was adapted with the least possible change."

It is quite clear that Justice Beatty did not have in mind any thought but that the lode mining regulations were founded on the placer rules that had just been established and that it was a natural step from the one to the other.[87] If he had entertained

---

[84] Jennison v. Kirk (1878), 98 U. S. 453, 457-8.
[85] Report of the Public Lands Commission (1880), pp. 395-402.
[86] Id. p. 396.
[87] J. Ross Browne entertained the same view, for in his report of 1867 on Mineral Resources, p. 231, he states that the early quartz regulations were framed "under the influence of persons familiar only with small claims customary in the placers."

any idea that the local lode laws were patterned after any system of mining law imported by miners from foreign countries, he would certainly have mentioned a fact of such unusual interest.

The mere failure of these three distinguished men, who were admittedly pre-eminent in their knowledge of the subject with which they were so intimately associated, to mention the fact that our lode mining law had a foreign origin, does not, of course, prove conclusively that it did not have some such basis. However, all fair minded persons must admit that such foreign influence if it actually existed must have been kept a profound secret, otherwise one or the other of these men would certainly have learned of it and called attention to it.

The main support for the idea that our lode law and its extralateral right was derived from foreign sources is to be found in Yale on "Legal Titles to Mining Claims, etc." Speaking of the origin of these rules and regulations he says:[88]

> "The real mining code, as far as it can be traced by legal ear marks, has sprung from the customs and usages of the miners themselves, with rare applications of common law principles by the Courts to vary them. Most of the rules and customs constituting the code, are easily recognized by those familiar with the Mexican ordinances, the Continental Mining Codes, especially the Spanish, and with the regulations of the Stannary Convocations among the Tin Bounders of Devon and Cornwall, in England, and the High Peak Regulations for the lead mines in the county of Derby. These regulations are founded in nature, and are based upon equitable principles, comprehensive and simple, have a common origin, are matured by practice, and provide for both surface and subterranean work, in alluvian, or rock *in situ*. In the earlier days of placer digging, in California, the large influx of miners from the western coast of Mexico, and from South America, necessarily dictated the system of work to Americans, who were almost entirely inexperienced in this branch of industry, with few exceptions from the gold mines of North Carolina and Georgia, and from the lead mines of Illinois and Wisconsin. The old Californians had little or no experience in mining. The Cornish miners soon spread themselves through the State, and added largely by their experience, practical sense, and industrious habits, in bringing the code into something like system. The Spanish-American system which had grown up under the practical

---

[88] (1867), pp. 58-9.

working of the mining ordinances for New Spain, was the foundation of the rules and customs adopted.

"Senator Stewart has ascribed undeserved merit to the early miners in pronouncing them the authors of the local rules and customs. . . . . . But they were not the spontaneous creation of the miners of 1849-50. Historical accuracy ascribes a different origin to them. They reflect the matured wisdom of the practical miner of past ages, and have their foundation, as has been stated, in certain natural laws, easily applied to different situations, and were propagated in the California mines by those who had a practical and traditional knowledge of them in their varied form, in the countries of their origin, and were *adopted*, and no doubt gradually improved and judiciously modified by the Americans. This self-evident fact can be admitted without detracting from our national pride."

Yale also gives General Halleck's opinion of their origin.[39]

"General Halleck ascribes to them a more limited origin, otherwise agreeing in the statement made. In his introduction to the translation of De Fooz, he says: 'But the miners of California have generally adopted, as being best suited to their peculiar wants, the main principles of the mining laws of Spain and Mexico, by which the right of property in mines is made to depend upon *discovery* and *development;* that is, *discovery* is made the source of title, and *development*, or *working*, the condition of the continuance of that title. These two principles constitute the basis of all of our local laws and regulations respecting mining rights.' (De Fooz, §§5, 7.)"

He concludes with a statement which more nearly embodies what is probably the real truth of the matter as far as the origin of these laws is concerned.

"An examination of the mining codes of different nations, tracing them back to remote antiquity, and through modern legislation, tested by the philosophical principles of comparative law, would, probably, result in the conclusion that they have a common origin, maintaining certain general equitable principles upon which all are agreed, and differing only in the details which a diversified ownership, the peculiarities of race, and condition of locality necessitate."

It seems quite certain that both Mr. Yale and General Halleck are mistaken in attributing the origin of these rules and regulations to Spanish influence. As already pointed out, the Spanish-Mexican mining laws were inoperative and unknown in

[39] Id. p. 71.

this new region at the time the early miners' laws were framed.[40] The requirements of discovery and development were universal requirements and were not characteristic of Spanish law alone.

Direct Germanic influence is also doubtful and the complex Germanic form of extralateral right is so different from the simple form of this right which developed in this country that the Germanic extralateral right could only remotely have suggested the idea here.[41]

Many writers attribute the source of our mining laws to Cornish influence. This idea does not seem well founded, for no extralateral right was exercised in the tin mines of Cornwall or Devonshire and the ancient right of tin bounding or right of staking out a mining claim on waste land had almost ceased to be exercised.[42] Most of the lode mining in Cornwall and Devon was carried on under leases from the Duke of Cornwall.[43] The fact that the Duke of Cornwall had the right to these mines and in leasing them, naturally, gave the lessee the right to follow the veins down indefinitely in depth and thus severed them from the surface, may have had something to do with the idea expressed in the early regulations here, that the vein was the principal thing and the surface a mere incident.

It cannot be denied, however, that the Cornish influence was pronounced. The early and widespread use in the miners' regulations of the term "lead" or "lode" and the appearance in these local rules of such terms as dips, spurs, angles, slides, fitters (flitters), leaders, dial (survey), offshoots is quite positive evi-

---

[40] 4 California Law Review, pp. 437-8; Hon. Charles T. Hughes, Jr., in his interesting article on "The evolution of Mining Law" (Vol. XXIV, Report of American Bar Association, p. 343) in summing up his views, has this to say on the Spanish influence: "The early miners, in their mountain gulches, in their humble cabins, at their primitive assemblages, unfamiliar with the history of mining laws and regulations in the old world, and even with the Spanish regulations which had prevailed in the very territory which they occupied, seized upon the aptest, wisest and most beneficial principles which could have been adopted, and by vigorous, strenuous, independent, but respectful assertion of their rights, secured their recognition at the hands of the general government, to the incalculable enrichment and advantage of the entire nation."

[41] Aguillon in his "Legislation des Mines, Étrangère" (1891), Part II, p. 292, in commenting on the American extralateral right, says: "It is, one realizes, the system of defining the claim by the ancient law, notably the German system of Langenfelder or Gestrektefelder."

[42] "Through the scarcity of wastrel land it (in bounding) has, however, become more or less obsolete." (Vol. II, Part I, p. 32) Transactions of the Mining Association of Cornwall.

[43] Bainbridge on Mines & Minerals (5th ed.), pp. 121, 133-134; Mac Swinney, The Law of Mines etc. (3rd ed.), pp. 176-177.

dence that Cornishmen supplied a large part of the mining vocabulary.

The resemblance of the extralateral right which was created by the miners here to the similar simple form of that right existing in Derbyshire, England, has led many to claim a direct relationship. This is doubtful, and unless some direct proof of Derbyshire influence can be adduced, the weight of evidence seems rather opposed to this view. If the Derbyshire influence had been pronounced, we would expect the Derbyshire term "rake," meaning vein, to have supplanted the Cornish "lode," and yet the word "rake" does not appear in any of the regulations.

If we examine the regulations themselves, the simplicity of the language employed, and the variations of expression used in the different districts to describe the same right, lead to the conviction that instead of being knowingly patterned after other mining codes, these local laws were merely the direct outgrowth of the necessities of the hour. It became necessary to apportion the placer ground among the increasing number of miners flocking into the mining districts and small square or rectangular areas of surface were naturally adopted as the size of claim to which each miner was entitled. But when veins became important it was equally natural for the miner to apportion the vein in short lengths and disregard the surface as something unimportant, for the vein was the thing of value. To follow the vein down on its dip to the extent that the miner owned of length was also a natural and normal sequence, for the miner was the discoverer of the top of the vein and why should he give up to another the vein on its dip when that other had nothing to do with finding it? Probably some such line of thought in the minds of these pioneers resulted in the adoption of their early rules regulating lode claims, including the extralateral right. That they did not have in mind any definite laws as a pattern granting the extralateral right to the locator, is further borne out by the fact that the extralateral right first appeared in the Saunders' Ledge regulations on June 6, 1851, in Nevada County, where the words "dips and angles" were employed to describe the right and one hundred feet in length on the ledge constituted a claim while, on June 7, 1851, only the day following, the miners of Drytown Mining District, Amador County, adopted regulations establishing the length of claims to be two hundred and forty feet in length of the vein "without regard to width" which was only another way of expressing the same idea that there was no limitation on the right to follow the vein in depth. Other regulations granting the same right to follow a certain length of vein indefinitely in depth were expressed in language which varied in each case. This diversity of expression to convey the same general idea of a right to follow down on the vein indefinitely and also the varying length of vein awarded to the locator in different districts, argue strongly against any idea of a definite prototype which influenced the drafting of these regulations.

The resemblance of many features of these regulations to the provisions of other systems of mining law is merely confirmation of the fact that if intelligent persons are confronted with a state of affairs creating a situation which demands regulation by a set of rules, they will frequently arrive at results similar in their broader aspects. Dictates of common sense will usually direct the adoption of rules based on equitable considerations. It seems quite certain that the pioneer miners of California proceeded along similar lines and met the situation which confronted them by adopting laws governing their mining operations, similar in many respects to other laws which had been evolved elsewhere under like circumstances. The similarity was a coincidence rather than the result of a deliberate recognition of pre-existing laws.[44]

Wm. E. Colby.

Berkeley, California.

---

[44] Walmesley in "The Mining Laws of the World" (1894), p. 163 says: . . . . . "The California system was probably not due to Mexican influence. The principle of possessory tenure, dependent upon continued work, is probably German in origin, and passed from Germany to other countries. Together with all the other peculiarities of the California system, it was adopted under the pressure of the peculiar circumstances of the case, a great rush of population to the gold-fields, more people than room for them, no courts, no surveyors, and an overwhelming necessity for simple right of property, based on priority and possession, and determinable by mere tape-line measurement, without surveying. These causes adequately explain the whole result." The basis of most of Walmesley's statements is the testimony given by Dr. Rossiter W. Raymond before the Royal Commission on Mining Royalties. (Third Report: England).

The presence here of foreigners in large numbers from all parts of the world lends weight to the idea that in a broad way, at least, certain fundamental principles may have been suggested by them to the original framers of these local codes, who may have thus been confirmed in their codification of similar ideas.

The Extralateral Right: Shall It Be Abolished?

IV. CONCLUSION.

Growth of Opposition.

WHEN the first concerted attempt to abolish the extralateral right was made is uncertain. The Act of 1866 was adopted without serious opposition to this feature.[1] It is true that Julien in the House of Representatives attacked this idea of granting a right "allowing one man to run half a mile under the land of another" but he did this because of his bitter opposition to the bill as a whole and not because he had any special information on the subject. Instead of representing mining sentiment in the West, he was the chief exponent of the plan which had taken such a strong hold in the East of selling or leasing the mines to the highest bidder and devoting the proceeds toward liquidating the national debt. His opposition to the extralateral feature was due to his general attitude of hostility to the desire

---

[1] William M. Stewart who has been so frequently and unjustly charged with forcing the federal mining Acts of 1866 and 1872 upon an unsuspecting public took a leading part in the Comstock litigation during the early 60's. " . . . . it was his plan to induce the different companies on the lode to put an end to otherwise certain litigation by defining their surface lines or the boundaries of their claims accurately and finally. . . . . When the boundary lines were determined it was to be stipulated that planes should be drawn perpendicular to these lines, extending indefinitely downward and that the mining operations of all companies should be confined within the limits of the planes bounding their respective claims. . . . . Now this was substantially a relinquishment of the cherished but litigious principle which allowed a locator to follow the dips of his ledge indefinitely, and a substitution of the often-decried Spanish or Mexican system of allotment. . . . . Unfortunately, the trustees of the Choller Company could not be persuaded to adopt Mr. Stewart's views, and he was reluctantly obliged to abandon his project and continue the fight." This role of Senator Stewart as champion of the vertical boundary system will surprise many who have ignorantly charged him with having originated the extralateral right idea in America. Comstock Mining & Miners by Lord Monograph, IV U. S. G. S., p. 145.

The Eureka mining district of Nevada on February 27, 1869, adopted a resolution declaring that the mineral in that district was found in the form of deposits rather than in true fissure veins or ledges and "Whereas this deficiency in the law may give rise to expensive litigations," square claims with vertical boundaries were adopted. Tenth U. S. Census, Vol. XIV, pp. 551-2.

of the West to have the long exercised right of free mining on the public domain recognized by positive legislation.

When the bill to amend the Act of 1866 was introduced in Congress in 1870 and 1871 and was finally enacted in 1872, no comment whatsoever was made on the extralateral feature during the course of the reported debates. Other provisions of the bill were extensively debated and altered but the section conferring the extralateral right remained unchanged and was not even criticised.[2]

Decided opposition to this feature of the mining law was definitely expressed, however, before the Act of 1872 had been in force many years. By Act approved March 3, 1879,[3] Congress authorized the appointment of a Commission to investigate the operation of the public land laws of the United States and make "such recommendations as they may deem wise in relation to the best methods of disposing" of such lands. A consideration of public mineral lands and the laws governing their disposition naturally came within the scope of the investigation of this Commission. This Commission made an elaborate report in 1880.[4]

Commenting on the creation of a new class of public lands in the United States; viz., mineral lands, resulting from the discovery of gold in California, the report states that the army of prospectors who roamed over the mountain ranges in quest of speedy wealth were not agriculturalists in search of homes but were composed of persons who desired to obtain title to mines.

> "As the region was a wilderness, and the authority of the general government was but imperfectly extended over the country, the miners framed for themselves regulations for their own government—crude, it is true, but in a general way securing justice. Under these local regulations or laws possessory rights to mineral lands were acquired which were afterwards confirmed by statutory law, and thus this second

---

[2] There may have been some discussion in committee but these proceedings were not reported and the fact that the elaborately worded apex section granting the extralateral right remained unchanged throughout all this discussion when other features of the bill were being radically amended and, as finally adopted in 1872, the fact that this section was identical in language with the corresponding section of the bill that had been introduced in the previous session of Congress, leads to the conclusion that there was then no serious opposition to the extralateral right.

[3] 20 Stats. at L. 394.

[4] Pub. Land. Com. Rep. (Washington, 1880), 690 pp.

class of lands was practically recognized in the administration of land affairs."

The Commission pointed out that if this land had been in private ownership the prospector would have been barred

> "and the mining industry which has so rapidly grown up in that country would have been delayed for years, perhaps for centuries. . . . .
> "Free exploration and the right to acquire property in mines by discovery led to the establishment of the great mining industries of the West. . . . . Thus a wise system of administering affairs relating to mining lands must recognize the importance of discovery in which poor men can engage. . . . . [5]
> "The United States mining laws of 1866 and 1872 are directly descended from the local customs of the early California miners."[6]

Investigating the operation of these mining laws which spread from California throughout the West and which "have stemmed the tide of Federal land policy and given us a statute book with English common law in force over half the land and California common law ruling in the other,"[7] the Commission called attention to the fact that east of the Missouri, mineral development was almost exempt from litigation growing out of conditions of the government conveyance of mineral lands while in the west it was "a history of the most frequent, vexatious, costly, and damaging litigation." .

> "There are two general features in the existing statutes which have provoked and directed the main lines of legal contest, and they are, first, the recognition by the law of the local customs and regulations; second, the attempted conveyance of a lode, ledge or deposit of rock in place bearing mineral, as a thing separate from and independent of the surface tract of ground, with the permission to follow such lode or deposit on its dip, even when in the downward course it passes beyond the side lines of the surface claim."[8]

Pointing out the magnitude of the evil of allowing the mining communities the right of local regulation, the Commission urged that this source of endless litigation should be promptly abolished by Congressional enactment.

---

[5] Id., pp. XIX-X.
[6] Id., p. XXXII.
[7] Id., p. XXXIV.
[8] Id., p. XXXV.

Taking up the second great class of evils, "those incident to the theory of the lode or ledge location," the Commission makes the following comment:

"It has proved in practice and in law that a lode or ledge is an absolutely indefinite thing, and the act of following this formation whose nature and limits can not be fixed beyond the locator's surface ground and under the surface ground of another owner, is the most frequent and vexatious cause of litigation."

This right to follow a lode into the ground of another works "a minimum of mischief in the case of a well defined fissure vein of regular course and dip."

"With such a defined fissure vein, by spending many thousand dollars and provided his cloud of expert witnesses are not tripped up by clever cross-examination, and the judge is impartial, and the jury are not corruptly influenced against him, after many months and perhaps years, during which his enterprise has been hand-cuffed with injunctions and himself reduced to poverty, the owner might derive whatever hollow comfort he could from a victory which left him ruined."[9]

"From this somewhat favorable working of the law" the Commission went on with the examination of other classes of cases involving complex vein occurrences and pointed out the impossibility of reconciling these with the practical workings of the law of apex.

"Your Commission, after a review of the lines of mining contests and a consideration of the complex nature of ore deposits, are unanimous in the conviction that any attempt on the part of the United States to convey such deposits as individual things beyond the vertical planes bounding the surface claim, must always end in a history of intolerable injustice."

It therefore recommended a repeal of the extralateral right and the substitution of the common-law system of vertical boundaries in its stead.[10]

The Commission submitted to Congress a draft of a proposed

---

[9] This is rather a sorry picture and while somewhat overdrawn would indicate that some at least of the Public Land Commission had come in contact with extralateral litigation.

[10] Pub. Land Com. Rep. (Washington, 1880), pp. XXXVII-XLI. The fact that this commission included in its number such eminent men as Clarence King, Thomas Donaldson, J. W. Powell and J. A. Williamson, gave this report more than ordinary weight.

Public Land law which contained among other provisions the following:

"Section 169.—Any mining claims located after the——day of — 1880, shall be bounded as to surface by straight lines, and all right to minerals contained therein shall be confined within vertical planes passing downward through said straight boundary lines."

"Section 170.—A mining claim located after — day of ——— may equal but shall not exceed a square of ——— feet on the side, and the same may be in any shape, so that neither length nor breadth shall exceed —— feet, nor the aggregate area exceed that of the square hereinbefore first described."[11]

Concerning the area of the common law mining claim the Commission made no recommendation since it had not received "a full expression of popular opinion," and that question was remitted to the legislative judgment of Congress.[12]

Assuming that it were desirable to abolish the extralateral right, this was the most favorable time to have eliminated it. The Act of 1872 had been in force only eight years and to have wiped out the law of apex at that time would have resulted in infinitely less hardship and readjustment than must inevitably follow if that right be abolished after the Act has been in force for nearly half a century. Since this report of the Public Land Commission was issued, the attempt to repeal this feature of the mining law has been urged at intervals.[13] In recent years this sentiment has increased to such a marked degree, and the abolition of the right is now advocated by so many distinguished mining authorities and leading mining associations[14] that the subject demands serious consideration.[15] Most of this agitation, however, has thus far been entirely too much engrossed with partisan condemnation of the law of apex, while but slight consideration has been given to the principles underlying the origin and exercise

---

[11] Id., p. LXXVIII.

[12] Id., p. XLI.

[13] See the files of the Mining & Scientific Press and Engineering & Mining Journal.

[14] Senate Document No. 233 (64th Congress, 1st Session). Report of Meeting of the Mining & Metallurgical Society of America in collaboration with the American Mining Congress, the American Institute of Mining Engineers, etc.

[15] There were several bills introduced in the 64th Congress, providing either for the outright repeal of the extralateral right or profoundly amending the mining law in many respects.

of the right and those features which furnish some measure of justification for its existence; and, most important of all, practically no thought has been directed to the consequences which must inevitably flow from an outright repeal. These consequences are exceedingly vital and far reaching and, unless the anti-extralateral advocates can furnish some practical solution which will minimize the mischief, the advocacy by many of them of outright repeal of the extralateral and discovery features of the mining law without a corresponding readjustment of our public land laws all along the line to meet this sweeping change, is going to produce results which will be most detrimental to the mining industry.

THE EXTRALATERAL RIGHT PRINCIPLE IS IDEAL IN THEORY.

It is generally conceded that the fundamental principle of the extralateral right is ideal in theory. The statements of those who have analyzed the situation surrounding the occurrence of lode or vein deposits and who have pointed out the lack of any essential relation between veins or mineral deposits in depth and the overlying surface amply support the principle of severance.[16] All that one has to do is to picture a vein dipping at an angle into the earth and visualize the result of vertical planes passed through surface boundaries cutting off the right to mine on the vein in depth at various points. Take the case where there are several veins dipping either parallel to each other or at varying angles and realize the complex condition that would result if overlying surface ownership controlled and vertical planes were projected downward to chop these veins up into segments of varying size and at different depths. Then conceive of the ideal condition under the extralateral law where the apex proprietor can follow a certain length of vein down indefinitely on its dip no matter where it leads. The practical result where veins are controlled by surface ownership and chopped up into segments of varying size and at varying depth is to bring about an attempt to consolidate the right to mine on the vein and thus sever the underground rights from the surface rights and make them independent of one another. Only by this means can veins be most economically operated. The intent of the extralateral law was to ac-

---

[16] 4 California Law Review, pp. 371-374, 388; 4 California Law Review, pp. 456-458.

complish this result in the first instance and avoid the necessity of subsequent consolidation, and hence the extralateral law is based on the fundamental conception of economic operation.

But, unfortunately, though the extralateral law is ideal in theory, it is far from ideal in practical results. If veins were ideal, with regular width and dip and strike, the extralateral law would work to perfection and no one could seriously advocate any change. Veins are, however, so complex in their occurrence with branches, faults, splits, junctions and every conceivable variation in strike and dip and width, and degree of mineralization, that no matter how well the law of the extralateral right may become settled, there will always be disputes arising over these physical vagaries.[17]

The candid investigator must admit that because of this situation the extralateral law is open to serious objection. Just how serious these objections are and whether they justify such drastic action as an outright repeal of this feature of the law will next be considered.

THE MAIN REASON FOR ELIMINATING THE EXTRALATERAL RIGHT.

If we analyze the arguments advanced by those who advocate abolishing the extralateral right, we find that they practically all resolve themselves into the objection based on an excessive amount of litigation.[18]

It has been assumed by most of these critics without investi-

---

[17] "We propose to abolish the law of apex not because the theory is objectionable but because the question of physical fact gives rise to never ending litigation." Victor G. Hills, in Transactions of American Institute of Mining Engineers, Dec. 1916, p. 2200.

[18] A critical examination of the statements made by those who are opposed to the retention of the extralateral right as reported at the meeting of the Mining & Metallurgical Society of America (Dec. 16, 1915) discloses that the main reason advanced for the repeal of the law was "continuous litigation," "uncertainties of title and litigation," "vexatious and most burdensome litigation," etc. See Senate Document No. 233 (64th Congress, 1st Session); also Bull. No. 91, Vol. VIII, No. 12, Mining & Metallurgical Society of America. See also the expressions of opinion contained in Transactions of the American Institute of Mining Engineers, Vol. XLVIII, pp. 368-371, in paper entitled "Why the Mining Laws Should Be Revised," by Horace V. Winchell.

Aguillon in Legislation des Mines Etrangere (1891), Vol. II, p. 292, mentions the historical lawsuits which have arisen in America through the right to follow mineral deposits downward indefinitely under adjoining surface.

"The law of the apex has proved more productive of expensive litigation than economical mining." Annual Report of Director of U. S. G. S. (1911), p. 15.

gation that extralateral litigation is a common occurrence in the various mining camps and has become a great burden which is seriously hampering the mining industry. A careful examination of the statistics leads one to believe that the real situation has been exaggerated. There has been much expensive litigation but it must also be borne in mind that because of the magnitude of the interests involved, such mining cases attract more than their due share of public attention.[19] Taking into consideration the immense importance of the mining industry and the fact that its operations are spread over such a vast territory in the West, the wonder is, not that there are so many extralateral cases arising, but that there are comparatively so few. A careful analysis of the law reports and tabulation of all extralateral cases appearing therein[20] indicates that during the years 1870-1916 inclusive, in all of the western states there has been an average of less than three extralateral cases per annum which have been reported.[21]

The reported cases do not, of course, include all the extralateral cases which have arisen within this period, but they do include the more important cases and afford a very reliable criterion of the proportion of cases arising in the various years. The tabulation indicates that the maximum of reported cases was reached in the year 1902 when ten cases were reported.[22] Since 1902 the number of reported cases has steadily decreased so that for the past decade, excluding duplications of the same case, extralateral litigation has not averaged two reported cases a year. During the years 1908 and 1911 there were no extralateral cases whatever reported.

The federal extralateral decisions of the trial courts usually find their way into the reports because of their importance. The extralateral decisions in the state trial courts are not found in

---

[19] In a similar way, because criminal trials are heralded with head lines in the daily press, it is little wonder that the erroneous idea is prevalent that the legal profession devotes the greater part of its time to criminal law.

[20] The writer acknowledges his indebtedness to Mr. Herbert C. Hoover for permission to use material which was tabulated at his request by Mr. Robert M. Searls of the San Francisco Bar. Mr. W. J. Aschenbrenner, also of the San Francisco Bar, has continued this tabulation to date.

[21] This estimate does not include the decisions on appeal from lower courts where the same case is reported below, since these appellate decisions would represent a duplication of cases already considered.

[22] Many of these arose out of the Heinze-Anaconda battles in Montana and most of the remainder were connected with the Cour d'Alene crop of litigation.

the reports but these cases are of such magnitude that they often reach the state appellate courts. The tabulation, therefore, includes practically all of the extralateral cases which have arisen during the past forty-five years, except the few cases which were not carried beyond the state trial courts. It is, of course, impossible to arrive at the exact number of these unreported cases and determine the percentage they bear to the reported cases, but judging from actual information obtained in many of the important western mining states, it is doubtful if the number of these unreported cases arising in the state courts would much exceed twenty-five per cent of the total number of reported cases. This would increase the average number of extralateral cases arising during the past forty-five years to slightly in excess of three cases per annum. Even assuming that the average number of unreported cases were equal in number to the cases actually reported, the total annual average would be less than six cases, with the past decade showing a material decrease even in this small number.

It would hardly seem that these few cases arising in the entire West, especially where an industry of such magnitude and importance as that of lode mining is involved, would justify the extravagant statements that have been made by some who urge the abolition of the right.[23] It must be remembered that this charge of excessive litigation is the main reason urged for repealing the "law of apex."

The deductions of the writer as to the comparatively small amount of extralateral litigation which has arisen, when we consider the vast number of lode mines being operated throughout the West under the extralateral law, is corroborated by an independent line of investigation made by Charles H. Shamel, the author of "Mining, Mineral & Geological Law." Proceeding along entirely different lines, he examined the syllabuses of all of the cases reported in Morrison's Mining Reports which contain all of the important mining decisions reported in the United States during the past half century. He arrived at the following result:

---

[23] The comparative infrequency of extralateral cases is illustrated by the fact that no extralateral case has yet appeared in the reports from Alaska, and thus far only one has been reported from Arizona. In California, which was the birthplace of the law of apex, the reported cases have averaged one for each three-year period during the past forty-five years. During the past decade there has been no reported case arising in California. Two unreported cases have been tried and decided in California during that period.

"I confess that I was surprised at the actual figures. The total number of syllabuses in the 22 volumes of decisions is 5,808, of which the number concerning the apex law is 115. The apex cases are only about 1.9 per cent of the whole. . . . . Instead of causing 99.9 per cent of mining litigation, as Dr. Raymond has somewhere stated, it has caused much less than its proportionate share of the trouble. Facts are stubborn things. The chief, the constantly reiterated, the convincing argument, against the apex law is based on a gross mistake as to the facts in the case."[24]

Hon. Charles S. Thomas, one of the United States senators from Colorado, who, as an eminent mining attorney is well qualified to speak on the subject of mining litigation, corroborates this view as to the ratio of extralateral cases as compared to general mining litigation. He says:

"Now the vast amount of mining controversy—and I am speaking of numbers of actions—has not been apex litigation. They have been the most expensive and the most far reaching. They have perhaps resulted in the greater proportion of injustice; but the conflicting (surface) locations have produced that multitude of cases, a small percentage of which perhaps reach the Court of Appeals, but whose aggregate has burdened the prospector and locator with an expense almost unbearable."[25]

It is not therefore an excessive amount of litigation which can be legitimately charged to the extralateral right, for the actual number of cases arising is surprisingly small—insignificant even, when compared with the vast number of claims exercising this right—but rather, the only valid charge on this score which can be made, is the great expense incident to such few cases as arise.[26] Valid criticism must be based on expensive litigation and not on the ground of excessive litigation.

PRACTICAL DIFFICULTIES OF REVISION.

The advocates of the repeal of the law of apex have given but little consideration to the serious consequences which will in-

---

[24] "Should the Apex Law be now Repealed?" Transactions of the American Institute of Mining Engineers, Vol. XLVIII, p. 312.

[25] Senate Document No. 233 (64th Congress, 1st Session), p. 65.

[26] The vast amount of costly litigation arising in the oil fields of California is strong proof that the vertical boundary system is not immune from this evil. Shamel cites the famous litigation involving vertically bounded zinc deposits in New Jersey, lasting for nearly half a century. Transactions of American Institute of Mining Engineers, Vol. XLVIII, p. 347.

evitably result unless other features of our public land law are simultaneously profoundly amended.

The greatest practical difficulty which will follow from abolishing the extralateral right and confining a locator to the mineral found within the vertical boundaries of his location, is the fact that only in those locations which embrace the apex of the vein can a discovery of mineral be readily made. Discovery of mineral within the boundaries of the location is the most vital essential of our existing mining law.[27]

Locations which include the apices or upper portions of the veins within their boundaries could still readily meet this important requirement of discovery, but surface locations overlying the dip of the vein at considerable distances from the apices or upper terminal edges of the veins could meet the discovery requiremnet only after the locators had expended considerable labor and time in sinking shafts to encounter the vein in depth. As the vein dipped further into the earth it would be increasingly difficult to make a discovery within the vertical boundaries of the overlying locations and finally at great depth the expense of sinking of such shafts would be absolutely prohibitive. It would be necessary under existing discovery requirements to sink vertical shafts on each surface location in order to perfect a discovery on each claim and there would be a consequent economic waste resulting from the expense of unnecessary duplication of such shafts. Under the extralateral law as it now exists a discovery on the apex of the vein is sufficient and the vein may be developed to great depth by a single shaft advantageously situated.

The consistent advocates of the abolition of the extralateral right cheerfully concede that this practical difficulty is a serious one and they are therefore forced to urge that the discovery re-

---

[27] "Discovery is the all-important fact upon which title to mines depends." Lawson v. United States Mining Co. (1907), 207 U. S. 1, 13, 52 L. Ed. 65, 28 Sup. Ct. Rep. 15. Discovery is the initial fact without which no rights to mineral lands can be acquired. Creede and Cripple Creek M. and M. Co. v. Uinta T. M. & T. Co. (1905), 196 U. S. 337, 345, 49 L. Ed. 501, 25 Sup. Ct. Rep. 266. Discovery is the source of title to mining claims and the first discoverer must be protected in the possession of his claim. "Otherwise, the whole purpose of allowing free exploration of the public lands for the precious metals would in such cases be defeated, and force and violence in the struggle for possession, instead of previous discovery, would determine the rights of claimants." Ehardt v. Boaro (1885), 113 U. S. 527, 535, 28 L. Ed. 1113, 5 Sup. Ct. Rep. 560.

quirement of our mining law be abolished also.[28] Those who are familiar with the main features of our existing mining law will at once appreciate that if these two fundamental features—discovery and extralateral right—are eliminated, that our system of American mining law built up as a result of the years of experience and intelligence of the practical pioneer miners will have been virtually emasculated. Very little more than an empty shell will remain.

Let us pause for a moment to examine critically just where this radical alteration will lead. Many critics have stated that the discovery requirement is a feature characteristic of American mining law exclusively and that it is a useless requirement unnecessarily suffered by the American miner. Both of these statements are erroneous. The discovery requirement is characteristic of most of the systems of mining law in the world.[29]

The elimination of the discovery feature from our law would wipe out the simplest and most practical form of test as to whether land is mineral or not. As the writer has already pointed out in an article discussing the proposal to abolish the discovery requirement,[30] it would be a grave mistake to eliminate this salutary provision from our law. Such elimination would destroy the simple test whereby mineral lands are now practically and easily classified under existing law so that mineral locators are able to readily defeat agricultural claimants desiring to obtain the same lands. The only alternative test that has been suggested would be to leave such classification to an appropriate branch of the Federal Government. Even this alternative would be open to serious objection. It would substitute the opinion of mineral experts and representatives of the Federal Government as to mineral character of land in place of the views of the practical miner; it would mean aggravating delays where mines were dis-

[28] "You cannot abolish the extralateral right without abolishing the right of discovery. They are all tied up together." Transactions of American Institute of Mining Engineers, Vol. XLVIII, p. 383.

[29] "Discovery in all ages and all countries has been regarded as conferring rights or claims to reward. Gamboa, who represented the general thought of his age on this subject, was of the opinion that the discoverer of mines was even more worthy of reward than the inventor of a useful art. Hence, in the mining laws of all civilized countries the great consideration for granting mines to individuals is *discovery*." Lindley on Mines, p. 335.

[30] "Revision of the Mining Law—Discovery," 3 California Law Review 191; Mining & Scientific Press (Feb. 7, 1914), Vol. 108, p. 246.

covered in rugged or desert regions remote from centers of travel; it would overturn a fundamental principle which was embodied in our mining laws by the pioneer miners, a principle which was already the heritage of ages of mining experience; and finally it would tear down and destroy to a large extent the great body of law that has gradually been built up with infinite patience and practical wisdom as a result of judicial interpretation operating through more than half a century. The law of discovery is now well settled and understood and to substitute for it an unknown and untried quantity would mean another period of uncertainty and litigation until a similar line of interpretative decisions had been rendered with respect to the new law. This superstructure of judicial interpretation is as important a part of the law and is as necessary for its satisfactory working as is the organic law which it interprets. It is even more important in one sense, for the organic law may be created "overnight" as it were, while the interpretation and harmonizing of this organic law, especially in its relation to other laws, necessarily takes years to accomplish.

Another practical difficulty to which the elimination of the extralateral right will give rise and which must not be overlooked is the fact that in certain of the western states condemnation of private rights of way for mining purposes is not permissible.[31]

The courts of these states have not taken the broader view followed in other states where it is held that the public welfare is so dependent upon the mining industry that a private mining operator can exercise the right of condemnation for rights of way for mining purposes.[32]

The practical effect of the abolition of the extralateral right in those states which deny the miner such a right of condemna-

---

[31] Inspiration Consolidated Copper Co. v. New Keystone Copper Co. (1914), 16 Ariz. 257, 144 Pac. 277; Consolidated Channel Co. v. Central Pacific R. R. Co. (1876), 51 Cal 269; Lorenz v. Jacob (1883), 63 Cal. 73; Amador Queen Mining Co. v. Dewitt (1887), 73 Cal. 482, 15 Pac. 74, County of Sutter v. Nicols (1908), 152 Cal. 688, 694, 93 Pac. 872; Const. of New Mexico, § 22; Const. of North Dakota, Art. 1, § 14; Const. of South Dakota, Art. VI, § 13; Const. of Washington, Art. 1, § 16, Art. XII, § 10.

[32] People v. District Court (1888), 11 Colo. 147, 17 Pac. 298; Baillie v. Larson (1905), 138 Fed. 177; Ellinghouse v. Taylor (1897), 19 Mont. 462, 48 Pac. 757; Dayton Gold and Silver Mining Co. v. Seawell (1876), 11 Nev. 394, 408; Overman Silver Mining Co. v. Corcoran (1880), 15 Nev. 147; Byrnes v. Douglass (1897), 83 Fed. 45; Strickley v. Highland Boy Gold Mining Co. (1906), 200 U. S. 527, 50 L. Ed. 581, 26 Sup. Ct. Rep. 301. For an excellent discussion of these divergent holdings, see Lindley on Mines, §§ 253-264.

tion would be to render him unable to operate as one mine two separated segments of the vein underlying two separated parcels of surface land owned by him where the intervening surface owner objected. Under existing extralateral law he has the right to follow his vein on its dip irrespective of surface ownership overlying the dip.[33]

Another consequence of the elimination of the extralateral right would be to make the ownership of overlying surface all important. Under existing law the extralateral claimant frequently is willing to make a material concession to his neighbor when it comes to a dispute as to the ownership of surface of a portion of his claim. If the surface in controversy does not include any portion of the apex of the vein, the surface right frequently does not assume sufficient importance to justify litigation and controversies are usually amicably settled or the surface proprietor bought out for a comparatively small sum. If the right to the vein should become entirely dependent upon surface ownership, as is the result where no extralateral right exists, it is obvious that surface title becomes so vital that surface disputes would materially increase in number and be contested far more bitterly than in the past. The inevitable result would be to create an additional crop of surface litigation to take the place of extralateral litigation.

Practically all of the states of the West have also legislated on the subject of mining law, supplementing the mining laws of Congress. Most of these have embodied in their legislation the extralateral provisions of the federal statutes. While action by Congress abolishing the extralateral right would doubtless have the effect of rendering these state statutes on the same subject inoperative, yet it would become necessary for each state to wipe this legislation off its statute books and harmonize its laws with the enactments Congress might see fit to substitute therefor.

The writer does not pretend to assert that these obstacles are insuperable, but calls attention to them for the purpose of showing that the repeal of the extralateral law is going to be attended by far-reaching results. No attempt has been made to exhaust the field of objectionable consequences which will flow from such a

---

[33] Lindley on Mines, § 568.

repeal and as a matter of fact many serious results would only become apparent years after the experiment had been put in operation.

Unavoidable and expensive litigation is admittedly a valid objection to the continued existence of the extralateral right. But we are not confronted by the simple situation which existed prior to the adoption of this right to follow the vein into the depth. If we could erase the slate and start anew in the light of our present day experience, there would be little room for argument that the vertical boundary system, while opposed to the natural economics of mining, would obviate much expensive litigation and on the whole be desirable. But, unfortunately, we can not start anew and we are confronted with the practical situation that during the past sixty-seven years there have been thousands upon thousands of claims located and patented under the law granting extralateral privileges with which we must reckon, as it is inconceivable that any rights already vested will be destroyed.

To have two fundamentally opposed systems of mining law operating side by side, one based on the principle of severance of mineral from the surface and the other based on surface ownership carrying with it the right to everything situated vertically beneath, would not tend to a simplification of our mining laws nor to their ready understanding by those who would avail themselves of their benefits, but would inevitably add an increasing number of problems to be litigated in the courts.[34]

The fact that the primary questions involved in the interpretation of the extralateral feature of the Mining Act have largely been set at rest by the Supreme Court of the United States is reflected by the diminishing number of cases involving extralateral rights which are presented to the courts each year, and this in spite of the continually increasing number of locations and operating mines where such questions might be raised. There are questions of extralateral right law still undetermined but these are becoming fewer in number each year. Most of the important

---

[34] "The apex theory of tracing title to a lode has led to much litigation and dispute and ought not to have become the law, but it is so fixed and understood now that the benefit to be gained by a change is altogether outweighed by the inconvenience that would attend the introduction of a new system." From President Taft's Speech at Conservation Congress, Minneapolis, Sept. 5th, 1910.

questions have been adjudicated. Because there are still some problems awaiting determination is not a valid reason for wiping out the great framework of judicial construction of the apex statute which has been built up during half a century.[35] Time will serve to eliminate virtually all of the questions of strict law which may arise over this subject but we cannot, of course, eliminate the questions of fact as to continuity and identity of vein occurrences which arise wherever complex vein conditions exist. Such extralateral questions will continue to arise and the great expense incident to the trial of these problems is admittedly a grave objection to the continued operation of the law of apex. But these cases will arise in any event in connection with rights already vested and a repeal of existing law will not eliminate any extralateral rights which came into existence theretofore.

Many of those who favor revision of our mining laws seem to have the idea that if a particular law gives rise to litigation all that has to be done to remedy the situation is to amend the law or substitute a new law in its place and that litigation will cease automatically if the proper kind of a substitute law is devised. Unfortunately, such an ideal result is seldom if ever attained in actual experience. Until the expression of ideas by means of language has been reduced to an exact science and all people think in the same terms, it is not possible for radical legislation to be enacted which will not in its turn have to run the gauntlet of attack based upon every conceivable ground that human ingenuity can devise.[36] The disposition of public mineral lands presents a complex problem and the dovetailing of such a law in with all the other public land laws is no easy task. In innumerable instances a new law must come in conflict with rights that have vested under the older mining law which it will supplant and we are certain to have a new crop of litigation that will

---

[35] "The large number and wide range of the decisions show that the value of mining laws depends on their status as established by the courts. . . . ." Annual Report of Director of the Bureau of Mines (1915), p. 35.

[36] "They [the elements of decision contained in the mining statute] are simple enough in expression but the contests of interest and ingenuity, induced or justified by physical conditions, have given rise to much litigation, and quite a body of jurisprudence has been erected in the exposition of the rights conferred by the statute. The number and fullness of the cases spare us much discussion." Stewart Mining Co. vs. Ontario Mining Co. 237 U. S. 350, 357-8.

unquestionably persist for years. The vital question is whether the benefits to be derived from a change in the law will eventually outweigh the hardships and uncertainties of this unavoidable period of statutory interpretation and readjustment.

A Suggested Remedy.

As a matter of fact the situation can be met in another way and valid criticism based on the expense of extralateral trials overcome to a large extent by reform in the present objectionable methods of handling such cases.[87] It is admitted that the reform would have to be radical but it is worth considering, for the extralateral right is bound to be the subject of adjudication in the future, as in the past, at least, as far as existing vested rights are concerned.

In each state there should be a provision added to its laws whereby a judge, specially qualified to try extralateral cases, could be called in to sit where such rights are involved. To the average judge an extralateral suit is like so much Greek and a large portion of the trial is taken up with educating the court on the elementary principles involved. Most of the mining laws of other countries recognize the fact that mining cases involve technical problems that can not be satisfactorily and intelligently adjudicated by the regular courts and, consequently, in practically all foreign countries a special tribunal is established to try mining cases.[88] In some countries jurors, even, are required to be experienced in mining.

Another objectionable feature which can be readily improved, is the present method of employment by each side of an army of experts.[89] Practically all extralateral cases resolve themselves,

---

[87] As Charles Shamel says: "The fault lies not with the apex law, but with the existing instruments and methods of legal procedure." Transactions of American Institute of Mining Engineers, Vol. XLVIII, p. 34.

[88] Any one who was familiar with the trial of mining cases in the federal courts before judges like Hawley or Hallett, who thoroughly understood these technical mining problems, will appreciate the great saving of time and expense which would result from the trial of technical cases by a specially qualified judge.

[89] The employment of experts in extralateral litigation is not an unmitigated evil. In many cases ore bodies of considerable value have been encountered as a direct result of litigation work or suggestions of the experts and in many mines the geological conditions are slighted and but poorly understood until an extralateral suit is instituted and then the first scientific information of value is obtained concerning a mining camp.

sooner or later, into a battle between opposing experts. This results in great expense as well as confusing exaggeration of structural details of minor importance. In a great majority of cases justice could be as readily obtained by a board of experts, one to be selected by each side and a third by the judge of the court, the expense to be shared equally by each party. These experts could examine the properties involved and make a report on the geological occurrences. They would agree on most facts, and where there was a difference of opinion litigation work could be ordered to further develop the points of difference. This plan would eliminate much of the expense and time consumed in such trials. The court would accept the facts agreed on as proven and confine the trial to disputed issues. This plan or some other framed along similar lines would do much to remove the stigma of an excess of expensive litigation to which the extralateral right is now properly subject. It would tend to minimize the existing evil which will still continue to abide with us in the case of all existing claims and would obviate a plunge into untried dangers and hazards which are bound to follow a radical change in our present law.

If it is litigation we wish to avoid, then why not also take up the question of compelling all locations in the future to conform to legal subdivisions.[40] By requiring lode claims to be located in conformity to public land surveys as is now required in the case of placers and also by registering all locations in the land offices, it will readily be seen that a vast amount of litigation arising by reason of conflicting surface rights would be eliminated. An amendment of the mining law as suggested would eliminate ten-fold as many cases as would be eliminated by abolishing the extralateral right. But by each of these remedies the advantage of economic operation of the ore deposit as a geological unit would be sacrificed. The vein on its dip into the earth has nothing in common with the surface and to parcel it out by surface area and vertical boundaries is a structural misfit and so would be the forcing of lode locations into rectangular surface areas conforming to the public land surveys. Such reforms are ideal from the standpoint of minimized litigation but

40 This is not a novel suggestion. See Transactions of American Institute of Mining Engineers, Vol. XLVIII, p. 422.

intensely impractical from the standpoint of the most economic mining of the ore deposits.

Most Countries Recognize Severance of Minerals From Surface.

One vital point must not be overlooked in this discussion. Most of the mining laws of other countries recognize severance from the surface itself of minerals lying underneath the surface.[41] The owner of the surface does not usually own the minerals lying in depth beneath his surface but a separate property exists in these underlying minerals which the state may grant to another person. As a result there is no serious conflict between the surface owner and the individual who is entitled to work the mineral deposits beneath the surface. The law of ownership of lands acquired on the public domain of the United States, on the contrary, only recognizes such severance to a limited extent.

Recent legislation by Congress does permit agricultural entry of lands valuable for coal, oil, gas, phosphates, nitrates, potash and other non-metallic minerals.[42] "Known lodes" are also excepted from placers[43] and "known mines" from townsites.[44]

The agricultural patentee is further safe-guarded in this country by a statute of limitations, which provides

> "that suits to vacate and annul patents thereafter issued shall only be brought within six years after the date of issuance of the patent.[45]

Not only does this statute of limitations operate to cut off a mining claimant's opportunity to acquire mineral already known to exist in patented agricultural ground but rulings of the Supreme Court of the United States and of various state courts have thrown additional protection around agricultural claimants so that after their *bona fide* entry on land under non-mineral public land laws

---

[41] Severance of underlying minerals from the surface and their segregation into distinct titles is characteristic of the laws of France, Belgium, Holland, Spain, Austria, Germany, portions of Italy, Greece, Norway, Sweden, portions of Russia, Canada, Australia, Japan, and most of Spanish America.

[42] See 3 California Law Review, p. 288, n. 45, in article entitled, "The New Public Land Policy."

[43] U. S. Rev. Stats., § 2333.

[44] U. S. Rev. Stats., § 2392.

[45] As to patents theretofore issued, the period of limitation was five years after the passage of the Act. Act of Congress approved March 3, 1891, 26 Stats. at L. 1093, § 8. See Lindley on Mines, § 784.

has been made, it is difficult for a mineral claimant to make a valid adverse entry on the same land.[46]

In other words, when the United States grants non-mineral title to land it is usually in practical effect an outright grant of all that the land contains. There is no dual ownership contemplated except in the few limited cases noted. Anyone who recognizes these advantages which the agricultural claimant now possesses in this country as against those desiring to acquire the mineral existing in the same lands, will appreciate to some degree, at least, the hardship which is going to result to the miner if the extralateral right is abolished without the simultaneous enactment of legislation designed to offset this difficulty. The inevitable result of an outright elimination of the extralateral right will be to feed all existing agricultural patents which have veins dipping beneath them with all such extralateral segments of such veins situated vertically beneath these agricultural patented lands, since such segments will fall by gravity into and become merged with the ownership of the overlying surface lands.[47]

Some may argue that this is a desirable result. It is doubtful whether the mine operator and prospector will enthuse over such an outcome. To allow minerals to pass into agricultural ownership is not going to facilitate the extraction of minerals from the soil. These two fundamental industries have many points of difference. The destruction of soil by actual removal thereof or deposit thereon of tailings, necessary in so many instances in actual mining operations, and the destruction of vegetation resulting from reduction and smelting processes has made the average agriculturist apprehensive and difficult to persuade that mining in his immediate vicinity is always for his best interests. Neither has the agriculturist any adequate conception of the true value of a mine and is inclined to place on the mineral existing within his ground an exorbitant and exaggerated price based on gross output. He does not take into consideration the vicissitudes of

---

[46] See Lindley on Mines, §§ 206-208, 77.

[47] While there is a difference of opinion on the subject, the weight of reason and views of the text writers support the contention that a miner who locates the apex of a vein within ground that is open to location, even though his location is made later in time than the date of the patent to agricultural land which overlies the dip of the vein, may follow his vein extralaterally underneath the prior patented agricultural surface. Lindley on Mines, § 612.

mining operations and the difficulties which must be overcome before a mine can be put on a paying basis. The abolition of the extralateral right will further fortify the farmer in this position and make him increasingly hard to deal with. With the extralateral right in existence, the agricultural surface owner can now be usually induced, for a small consideration, to part with any claim he may assert to underlying mineral rights, for he is aware of the right of the lawful apex proprietor to follow the vein and penetrate beneath his land without his consent. It will be quite a different matter to deal with him when he realizes that he has become the actual and undisputed owner of the vein situated vertically beneath his surface.

The Extralateral Right is Based on the Principle of Severance.

The main exception in the public land law of the United States existing today which takes the place of severance in other countries, is the right of the owner of a valid lode location embracing the apex of a vein to follow the vein extralaterally underneath adjacent surface. In other words, the extralateral feature of American mining law operates to segregate mineral deposits in the nature of lodes or veins from the surface land overlying the dip of such veins or lodes.[48] The practical result of abolishing the right to follow a vein extralaterally and confining the locator to his vertical boundaries and of also abolishing the discovery requirement would be that agricultural claimants could readily file on and enter upon land overlying the dip of the vein. Under our existing land laws there is no way to prevent such action unless the Land Department can be persuaded to withdraw the land from agricultural entry pending its classification which would be manifestly impossible in every instance, as well as interfering with bona fide acquisition of agricultural titles. With the extralateral law in force, the locator can locate a claim embracing the apex of the vein and make a valid discovery on the portion of

---

[48] "The Act of 1866 was in effect a proclamation severing veins and lodes of the character specified from the body of the public domain. It was the announcement of a governmental policy, whereby ledges within the earth were to be considered as distinct entities, and to be dealt with as such in administering the public land system. This policy has never been entirely changed. In the main it is as much a part of the existing system as it was of the one which it succeeded." Lindley on Mines, § 568.

the vein which is nearest to the surface. This serves to carve out the vein on its dip beneath agricultural land and it is usually immaterial whether the agricultural claimant acquires title to the surface overlying the dip or not. Abolish the extralateral right and it becomes difficult and in many cases impossible to discover mineral within the vertical boundaries of claims overlying the dip of the vein. Agricultural claimants might be first on the ground and under the land laws as now interpreted they could prevent prospective locators 'from coming on the ground for the purpose of making a discovery. As already pointed out, discoveries perfected by sinking shafts to encounter the vein in depth, even if made without opposition, become economically wasteful and undesirable.

The Only Logical Alternative is to Sever Minerals From Surface.

After giving this subject serious consideration for a number of years it is the writer's deliberate opinion that, if any change is to be made in existing law and if conditions are to be improved rather than made worse, instead of abolishing the extralateral right principle, it should be carried even further by amendment of our public land laws providing for the severance from surface lands of all minerals except superficial deposits. Surface lands could be disposed of under existing laws providing for the acquisition of agricultural and other non-mineral titles except that the mineral should be permanently reserved from such surface grants. As the law now stands, and as has already been noted, only minerals known to exist at the date of the agricultural grant are reserved and even such minerals become the property of the surface proprietor by virtue of the existing statute of limitations and also the additional protection thrown by the courts about a surface proprietor in possession.

By reserving minerals from agricultural lands and allowing the miner the right of entry for purposes of prospecting under restrictions with the added requirement that the surface proprietor be compensated for damage, the interests of both the miner and the agriculturist would be conserved. In all the important mining countries of the world this segregation has taken place and this is the reason why in such countries the extralateral principle is not essential, whereas, in the United States, without such segregation or severance of minerals from the surface, the extralateral right has a most powerful additional reason for existence. With severance of minerals and segregation of agricultural and mineral interests, the element of discovery also, now so vital in the mining law of the United States, would assume secondary importance. Discovery instead of being of prime importance, as of necessity it must be under existing law where no segregation of minerals from the surface exists, could be made a secondary requisite, only required after the mineral locator had plenty of time in which to make a discovery, taking into consideration the difficulty of so doing in particular cases. If the principle of severance is incorporated in a revised public land law, a vertical boundary system for the acquisition of mineral lands could be simultaneously adopted without resulting in great hardship to the miner, for the agricultural surface claimant could no longer claim the underlying minerals. The surface perimeter within which the miner could work should be so adjusted as to give him as much opportunity as possible to mine in depth on the vein. This would in effect be an adoption of the French system of mining law. However, a radical change of this sort would unquestionably result in increased supervision of mining operations by the Federal Government and conversely a material sacrifice of individual control over such operations.[49] It might even result in permanent reservation by the Federal Government of all minerals, both metalliferous as well as non-metalliferous, and their disposition under a leasing system. This would be in line with the new public land policy as evidenced by recent acts of Congress and of the executive branch of the government which have been upheld by the United States Supreme Court.[50]

Whether such segregation is at this late day practical is a question that can only be determined after it has been thoroughly considered from every standpoint. As already noted, the Federal Government has provided for such severance in the case of lands containing coal, oil, gas, phosphate and similar minerals and it may be that the experience derived from the practical development of such lands will aid in determining this serious problem when applied to the metalliferous minerals.

---

[49] This is conspicuous in the administration of the French mining law. 4 California Law Review, pp. 373-374.

[50] 3 California Law Review, pp. 269-291.

The suggestion that severance of minerals from the surface will solve many of the difficulties standing in the way of the outright abolition of the extralateral right is not new. The logic of the situation has caused others to advocate the change.[51]

The severance of surface title from the underground minerals would also discourage speculators and blackmailers who now fraudulently seek to acquire title to surface lands under agricultural laws in order to levy tribute upon the bona fide mining operator. There are many problems that would have to be carefully considered if such a material change were made in our

[51] "The one great thing which would do away with all of our troubles on the discovery question, and also a lot of other mining law troubles, is the divorce of surface and mineral titles. . . . . The use of the surface and the extraction of minerals do not, except to a limited extent, naturally belong together, and any law which persists in keeping the two inseparable must be full of injustice and trouble brooding." Victor G. Hills in Transactions of American Institute of Mining Engineers, (Dec. 1916), p. 2202.

An able paper entitled "The Segregation and Classification of the Natural Resources of the Public Domain," by Frederick F. Sharpless appears in the Transactions of the American Institute of Mining Engineers, Vol. XX, pp. 386-400. The author points out the many advantages of segregating the surface from the mineral title and calls attention to the fact that: "In nearly all of the Provinces of Canada, there are three distinct rights in every parcel of land—timber rights, mineral rights and agricultural rights. . . . . In Australia, the segregation of surface from mineral rights has been the custom in most of the colonies for many years. . . . . While segregation of surface from mineral rights would not cure all existing difficulties connected with our present mining laws, it would, because of the very different nature of these rights, simplify the application of remedies."

After the main report of the Public Land Commission had been submitted to Congress, Maj. J. W. Powell, one of the Commission, qualified his approval of the report by adding a provision in the case of certain agricultural lands classified by the commission as pasturage lands, that "all subterranean mining property and rights for mining purposes, are hereby severed from the surface property," and that in the case of all such patents issued, the same reservation should be inserted and the property "shall be servient to the easements necessary for discovering and working mines therein." He also urged that in the case of mineral lands every patent should have inserted the following clause: "Except and excluding from these presents all surface property rights, provided that there shall be dominant in the property conveyed in this patent the easements on the surface property necessary for discovering and working mines therein."

The Commission had recommended that lands more valuable for mineral than agricultural purposes should be classified as mineral lands and subject to sale and entry only under mineral laws. Major Powell argued that since one-half of the mineral lands in the western United States were forest lands from which, under the Commission's recommendation, the timber alone was to be sold to timber claimants, thus leaving such lands open to mineral exploration, and since the other half of the mineral lands were largely pasturage lands, that this severance recommended by him would quite thoroughly protect the mining industry.

mining law, but the experience of other countries which have successfully operated their mines under laws based on this principle would afford great assistance in framing such legislation.[52]

The complex problem here presented is surrounded with profound difficulties and no matter in which direction we turn, we are confronted with unknown quantities and untried conditions. Any critic who ventures to prophesy with any degree of assurance that, by abolishing the extralateral right and also the time-honored principle of discovery, the millenium in mining operations will be attained, has closed his eyes to these uncertainties and is acting on blind faith. The writer does not claim to have received any information from an inspired source and is free to confess that the more the situation is studied the graver its uncertainties become. It will take a master mind to hew the way and devise a substitute law which will work in harmony with our other land laws and which will not bring chaos in its wake.

A commission composed of the best talent available has been proposed but legislation to bring about this result failed at the last session of Congress. It is certain that if revision is desirable it should not take place piece-meal and without due consideration of its effect on other land laws.[53]

---

[52] "An enlightened public sentiment concerning our mineral land policies can be formed only in the light that is afforded by knowledge of the kindred systems of the progressive peoples of the earth." United States Senator Thomas J. Walsh, Transactions of American Institute of Mining Engineers, Vol. XLVIII, p. 411.

[53] The provisions of the proposed Revision Commission Bill were explained at length in Transactions of the American Institute of Mining Engineers, Vol. XLVIII, pp. 405-411. Unquestionably, the plan there urged of general revision rather than "tinkering or patchwork revision" cannot be successfully controverted. Writing of the present laws, Edmund H. Kirby there says (p. 406): ". . . . Their various parts are so interdependent that it is practically impossible to correct individual faults without revising the laws as a whole."

There were several bills introduced in the 64th Congress having for their object the revision of the mining law. One in particular (Senate 42) provided for an outright repeal of the extralateral right without any attempt to revise other features of the law so as to minimize the hardships that would inevitably result. The opinion of the Department of the Interior was requested and Secretary Lane on Jan. 21, 1916, wrote the Chairman of the Senate Committee on Public Lands as follows: "It is certainly undesirable to attempt revision by partial and piecemeal methods. The entire mining field should be surveyed and the existing mining statutes revised only after thorough examination in all particulars. This can be best accomplished by a commission such as is contemplated. In view of the probable creation of such a commission, whose duties will include consideration of the very matters included in the present bill, Senate 42, I deem it inadvisable to make any comment upon the merits of the proposed

The writer feels justified in asserting that the following summarized statements are amply supported by the facts presented in the course of this discussion:

1. The extralateral right principle has existed in one form or another in many of the mining laws of the world but in nearly all instances this feature has been eventually abolished because of the litigation and uncertainty which it produced.

2. The extralateral right was adopted as a part of the mining law of the West by the pioneer miners when they made their earliest quartz locations in 1850 and 1851 and it became the almost universal custom and usage of the miners throughout the mining districts to exercise "dip rights."[54]

---

measure, and would suggest that the matters there involved be left to the careful study and consideration of such commission. I accordingly recommend at this time that Senate 42 be not enacted."

[54] Dr. Rossiter W. Raymond, who was intimately associated with the development of the mining law of the public domain, has contributed many learned and illuminating articles on the general subject and particularly on "The Law of the Apex" (Transactions American Institute of Mining Engineers, Vol. XII, p. 387) which descriptive phrase as well as the term "extralateral," he introduced into the literature of American mining law. He calls attention to the fact that "the term 'extralateral' could not have been applied under the Act of 1866," for the reason that the locator was entitled to a certain length of vein without regard to any width of surface ground. (Transactions of American Institute of Mining Engineers, Vol. XLVIII, p. 302). In other words, the miner's surface claim was not restricted under the Act of 1866 by lateral boundaries and hence extralateral pursuit of the vein would necessarily be a misnomer. The "dip right" as applied to this early appearance of the right to follow down indefinitely on the vein is technically a more accurate use of terms. ("The 'dip right' of the early miner was the forerunner of the modern extralateral right." Lindley on Mines, § 566). However, this differentiation of terms is more or less academic, for as a matter of fact, most of the early local rules and customs of the mining districts (See 4 California Law Review, pp. 448, 449, n., p. 47) and many of the territorial legislatures (See id., pp. 450-452) prescribed a definite lateral surface boundary limitation for lode claims and even in those districts where no such limitation was imposed, the location and occupation of all the available surface territory in the vicinity of important mines necessarily resulted in a definite lateral surface limitation for each lode claim and under such circumstances it is not a misuse of words to apply the term "extralateral" to the right that the miner exercised even in the earliest days. The same may be said of the use of the phrase "the law of the apex." Dr. Raymond points out (Transactions of American Institute of Mining and Engineering, Vol. XLVIII, p. 302; also Vol. XLIV, p. 61) that the word "apex" first appeared in the Act of 1872. As a matter of fact the apex or upper terminal edge of the vein was just as essential and its possession constituted the prime basis of the miner's right to follow the vein down on its dip in the early 50's and under the Act of 1866 as under the Act of 1872, which expressly called it by name. All of the extralateral cases decided under the Act of 1866 bear out this statement.

No attempt has been made in the course of this discussion to keep

3. The legislatures of practically all of the western states and territories had by statute declared the extralateral right to be the mining law in force in their respective jurisdictions when Congress passed the Act of 1866 which adopted and crystallized this miner's law without material alteration.

4. The Act of Congress of 1872, which is still in force, further codified and confirmed this miner-made law, changing it only in minor respects and leaving the fundamental principle of extralateral pursuit substantially as the miners had originally adopted it.

5. The law of discovery is not only handed down to us by the pioneer miners of the West but is also a heritage of centuries of mining experience throughout the world.

6. To abolish the extralateral right will result in forcing the abolition of the principle of discovery as applied to lode mines as well, and these are two of the most vital features of our mining law.

7. With the extralateral right repealed, the only important feature of our law which has the effect of severing the underlying mineral from the surface will have been eliminated and with the principle of discovery eradicated, the simple and practical test, now thoroughly understood, will no longer be available to the prospector and locator, and unless some substitute is furnished he will find himself at the mercy of the agricultural claimant or the unscrupulous speculator.

8. The alternative suggested of leaving classification of lands to government agents will shift the initiative in determining mineral character from the individual locator, as it exists at present, and will be a long step in the direction of complete government control of metalliferous mining.

9. The logical solution based on world experience is to sever all mineral except superficial deposits from the surface and dispose of the minerals and the surface separately.

10. Whether a workable system based on this principle of severance can be devised at this late day which will not result

---

this refinement of terms in mind for it would serve no practical purpose and would merely result in confusion. The expressions "extralateral right," "law of apex," and "dip right" have been used to convey the same general idea of a right to follow a certain length of vein on its dip into the earth indefinitely.

in producing greater confusion and more litigation by reason of new and untried problems and conflict with innumerable rights vested under the former system, is a question which would tax the wisdom of Solomon.

11. In any event, revision, if attempted, must be general and not piecemeal and should be enacted only as the result of the most careful deliberation by a commission composed of the best talent available.[55]

Wm. E. Colby.

Berkeley, California.

---

[55] On April 4, 1917, Senator Smoot introduced in the United States Senate (S. 104) a bill "To provide for a commission to codify and suggest amendments to the general mining laws," with power "to hold public hearings in the principal mining centers in the Western United States and Alaska," etc., and to "consider the laws and experience of other countries with respect to disposition and development of mines and minerals" and "within one year" to submit to the President a report and "a tentative code of mineral laws."